# MY BRILLIANT BIG ACTIVITY BOOK

CARLTON KiDS

# what's inside this book?

## Things to make

Make an alien mask on page 18, monster feet out of cardboard boxes on page 27, or some purple ooze on page 130!

## Things to draw

Decorate some sunglasses worthy of a pop star on page 31, paint a dragon's nails on page 173 and copy a dancer into the frames on page 177.

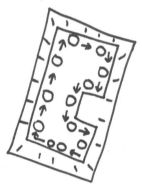

## Puzzle fun

Finish the jigsaw on page 39 and work your way through the maze on page 41!

## Stories and pictures

From pirate comics to complete on page 25 to reading all about star constellations on page 98, this book is filled with stories to read.

This is a Carlton book

Text, design and illustration copyright © Carlton Books Limited 2018

Published in 2018 by Carlton Books Limited
an imprint of the Carlton Publishing Group,
20 Mortimer Street, London, W1T 3JW

A catalogue record is available for this book from the British Library.

10  9  8  7  6  5  4  3  2  1

ISBN: 978 1 78312 367 4

Printed and bound in China

**Authors:** Mandy Archer, Andrea Pinnington, William Potter, Penny Worms
**Executive Editor:** Alexandra Koken
**Junior Designer:** Kate Wiliwinska
**Illustrations:** Zdenko Basic, Leo Brown, Andrea Castellani, Smiljana Coh, Chris Gould, Adam Larkum, Stuart Martin, Dud Moseley, Jennie Poh, Anna Stiles, Manuel Sumberac, Elle Ward, Rebecca Wright
**Production:** Emma Smart
**Photos:** Thinkstock.com and iStockphoto.com

# POTTY PYRAMID MAZE

This sightseer has taken a fascinating pyramid tour in Egypt, but she's got lost!

Help her find a way back to the exit before the sun goes down.

THE WORLD'S MOST FAMOUS PYRAMIDS STAND IN GIZA, NEAR EGYPT'S NILE RIVER. EACH ONE IS A TOMB FOR AN ANCIENT EGYPTIAN KING.

EXIT

TOUR BUS

4

The answer is at the back of the book.

# Cruise views

Ship ahoy! What can you see through the ocean liner's porthole?

Draw your view here.

Congratulations!
Only first-class passengers get a cabin with a window.

Copy each step-by-step drawing into the boxes below.

First, draw an oval for her head, then two shapes like these ones for her body.

Now, give her a neck, some little sleeves, then draw in the tops of her legs.

Good start!

Getting there!

Try drawing some more style queens in colouring pages in this book!

Next, give her a high pony tail, some arms, a belt and some stylish boots.

Finally, draw in her face, decorate her clothes and give her some accessories!

Almost done!

GREAT WORK!

# SPOOK SPOTTER

Ghosts need friends too.

Show how good a ghost spotter you are by matching the eight pairs. Draw lines between them.

The answers are at the back of the book.

# SPELLING SPREE

Finish writing this spell from an ancient book of magic. You can choose from the list of words and pictures supplied, or make up your own.

## Spell to turn a person into a _____

First heat up a cauldron of _____. When it begins to boil drop in a live _____. Stir in a large spoonful of _____, a pinch of _____, the eyes of a _____ and six bones from a _____. When the mixture smells of _____ pour in a cup of _____ blood and sprinkle a dozen wings off a _____ and a scraping of _____. Wave your wand in the shape of a _____ above the smoke, stamp three times on the ground, and say the magic word "_____". Add a thimble of the potion to your victim's drink. Then watch him turn _____ and start _____ like a _____.

alacazam
beetle
burping
cheese
claw
earwax
eyeball
fly
frog
green
hair
hopping
intestine
jumping
lizard
monster
newt
poison
presto
rat
rotten eggs
scab
slime
smelly
spider
stink
teeth
toad
tongue
vampire
vein
venom
wart
werewolf

# Let's make some noise!

Join the dots to find out which
instrument this noisy pop star is playing.

The answer is at the back of the book.

# The show must go on!

Help this leading lady to find her way to centre stage!

Finish

Start

The answer is at the back of the book.

11

# Seeing things

There are 10 differences between these pirate pictures.
Can you spot them all?

# Naming knights

## What would you be called if you were a knight?

Take the name of your first pet
(use someone else's if you didn't have one)

.......... Simba ..........

(Nutty-Noddle, Whisky, Tiddles, Mouse?)

How are you feeling?

.......... Tired ..........

(grumpy, clever, proud, happy?)

What's your lucky number?

.......... Thirteen ..........

(125, 31, $4\frac{3}{4}$, 27, 1?)

Arise, Sir Simba Tired The 13th ..........

(Nutty-Noddle, Grumpy the 27th?)

# Name that baby!

Puffy
..............................

Speedy
..............................

Shakey
..............................

blocky
..............................

What do you think these cute baby
dragons are called?

# Firework fantasy

Draw some more celebration fireworks to light up the sky above the Palace.

Fizz!

Bang!

Whizz!

Boom!

# Mirror, mirror!

Draw what you can see in the magic mirror.
Is it the fairest of them all?

17

# HOW TO MAKE YOUR ALIEN MASK

**1.** Carefully cut out the mask and eyeholes, following the dotted lines.

**2.** Cover the holes marked at each side of the mask with sticky tape to reinforce them.

**3.** Push a pencil through the marked holes.

**4.** Thread string or elastic through the holes and knot it in place, so that the mask fits snugly on your head.

18

# GALAXY GAGS

Colour in the scenes
and fill in the word balloons
to create your own jokes.

19

# Ready to wear

Design an outfit for every season of the year.

Spring sensation

Summer sizzler

Autumn arrival

Winter wonder

# Me time!

Fill the shelves and dressing table with your favourite beauty things.

jewellery stand

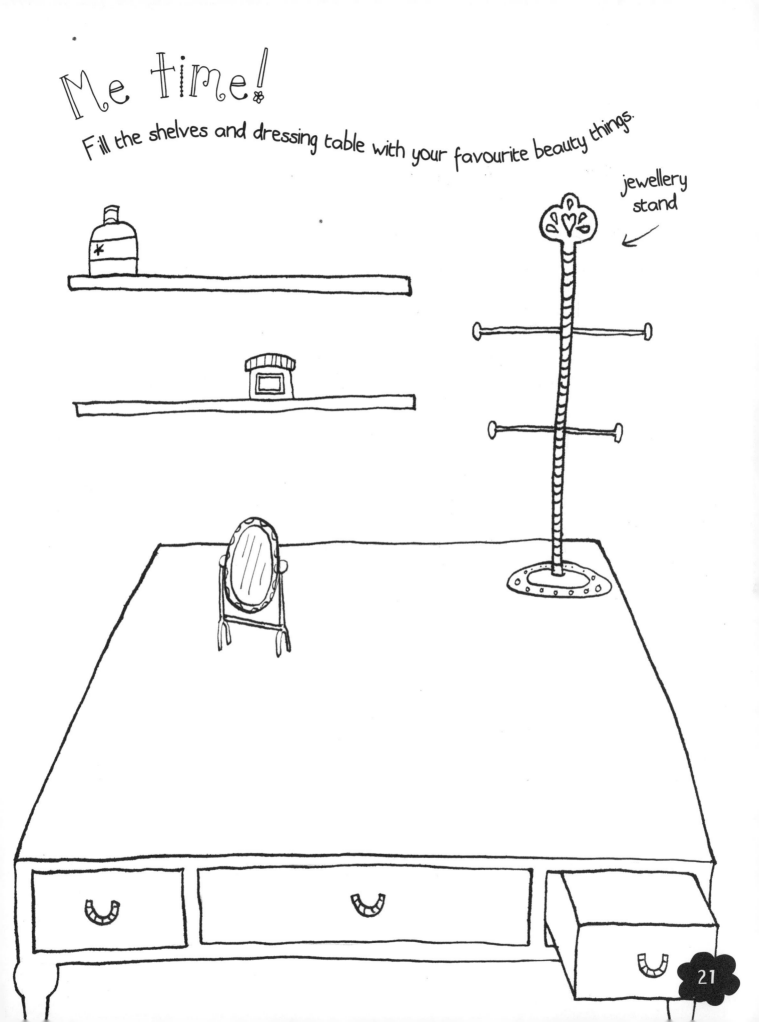

# Sandcastle art

Copy this sandcastle onto the empty grid opposite.

It's easier if you copy the lines square by square.

# Bearded buccaneers

Draw some beards and moustaches on these crazy pirates!

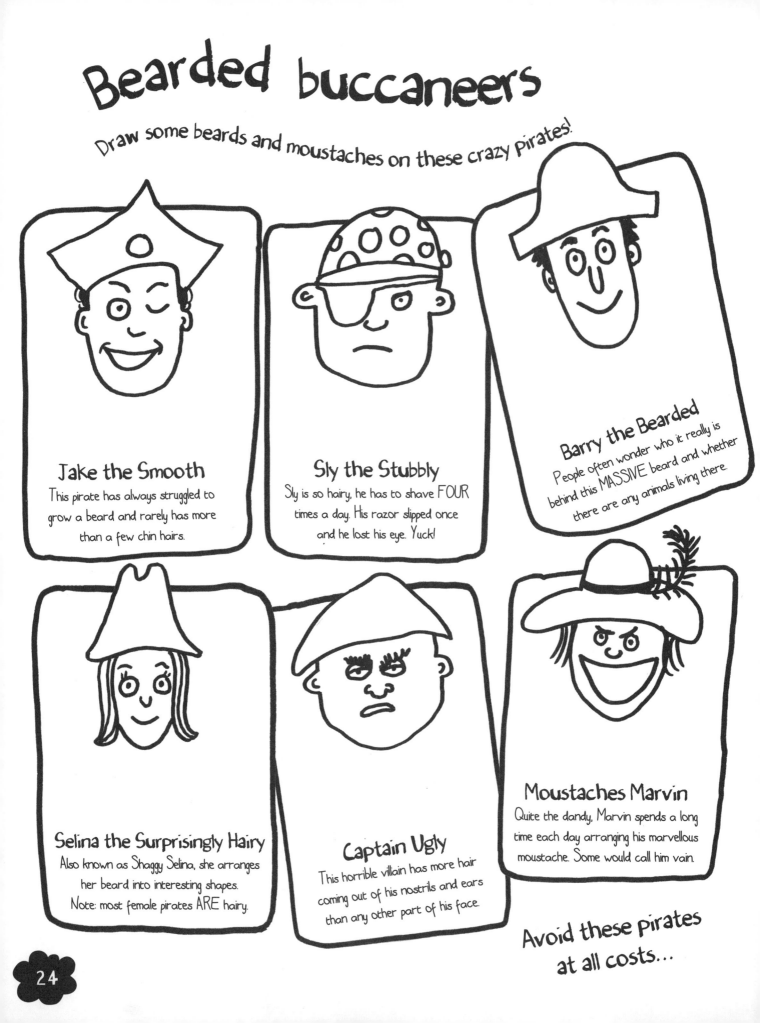

### Jake the Smooth
This pirate has always struggled to grow a beard and rarely has more than a few chin hairs.

### Sly the Stubbly
Sly is so hairy, he has to shave FOUR times a day. His razor slipped once and he lost his eye. Yuck!

### Barry the Bearded
People often wonder who it really is behind this MASSIVE beard and whether there are any animals living there.

### Selina the Surprisingly Hairy
Also known as Shaggy Selina, she arranges her beard into interesting shapes. Note: most female pirates ARE hairy.

### Captain Ugly
This horrible villain has more hair coming out of his nostrils and ears than any other part of his face.

### Moustaches Marvin
Quite the dandy, Marvin spends a long time each day arranging his marvellous moustache. Some would call him vain.

Avoid these pirates at all costs...

# Ripping yarns

Make up your own pirate story using these pictures.

Draw in the ending to your story.

... and he/she/they lived happily ever after! (circle the right word)

# BRILLIANT BATS

Invite a colony of bats to your Halloween party with this ghoulish garland.

**1.** Copy the bat designs several times onto black card and cut them out. You could fold the paper to cut out several bats at once.

**2.** Carefully pierce holes for the eyes and on the wing tips, as marked. You could use a hole punch or push a pencil through the paper into modelling clay.

**3.** Thread your bats onto a length of string. Alternate the bats as you go along. Hang the garland in the party room.

# FREAKY FEET

Something weird is afoot! Here's how to make your own wacky werewolf feet to stomp around the neighbourhood.

**YOU WILL NEED:**

Two empty tissue boxes big enough to fit on your feet

Brown or white fake fur, or paint and paintbrush

Glue, scissors and green craft foam or cardboard

1. Draw around each side of one tissue box to measure out enough fur to cover both boxes. (If you don't have fake fur, you can paint your boxes with hairy monster patterns or scales.)

2. Make the claws. Cut out six foam or cardboard triangles with a flap at the base of each. Attach three claws to each box by gluing the flaps so that the claws protrude from the end of the box. Glue the fake fur to the boxes, making sure that the claws are sticking out and leaving the holes free for you to slip your feet in.

3. Stuff the boxes with spare foam or newspaper as padding for your feet. When the glue is dry you can put on your freaky feet and go out howling!

# spot the difference

There are ten differences between these two pictures of Snow White and the queen. Can you find them all?

The answers are at the back of the book

# cloakroom catastrophe

These actresses are about to hit the red carpet, but there's been a mix-up in the cloakroom.

Can you help them to find their handbags before the movie premiere begins?

The answers are at the back of the book.

# sparkling shades

pop stars keep a low profile
by hiding behind huge sunglasses.

Here are some
sunglasses for
you to decorate.

# STRETCH AND SQUASH

## What would people look like if they lived in stronger or weaker gravity?

**EARTH**

### WHAT IS GRAVITY?
Gravity is the force that makes things fall to the ground and stops us floating away from Earth. On some huge planets, like Jupiter, gravity is stronger than on Earth, which would make you feel almost three times heavier. On Mars, it's lighter, so we could leap three times as high into the sky.

**MARS**

Copy the astronaut as a squashed, heavier person on Jupiter and as a tall, lighter person on Mars, with much less gravity.

**JUPITER**

# FRIENDLY FACE

A space probe has received a picture from the edge of the galaxy. Follow the guide to colour in the grid squares and reveal it!

**Colour these in black:**
ROW A: 6, 7, 8, 9, 15, 16, 17, 18
ROW C: 6, 8, 10, 12, 14, 16, 18
ROW E: 12
ROW F: 11, 12
ROW G: 1, 2, 22, 23
ROW H: 2, 22
ROW I: 1, 2, 6, 8, 10, 12, 14, 16, 18, 22, 23
ROW M: 8, 10, 12, 14, 16
ROW P: 8, 9, 10, 11, 12, 13, 14, 15, 16

**Colour these in yellow:**
ROW C: 7, 9, 11, 13, 15, 17
ROW I: 7, 9, 11, 13, 15, 17
ROW K: 6, 7, 17, 18,
ROW L: 6, 8, 9, 10, 11, 12, 13, 14, 15, 16, 18
ROW M: 6, 18
ROW N: 6, 8, 9, 10, 11, 12, 13, 14, 15, 16, 18
ROW O: 6, 18
ROW P: 7, 17

**Colour these in green:**
ROW B: 5, 6, 7, 8, 9, 10, 11, 12, 13, 14, 15, 16, 17, 18, 19
ROW C: 4, 5, 19, 20
ROW D: 4, 5, 10, 11, 12, 13, 14, 19, 20
ROW E: 4, 5, 10, 13, 14, 19, 20
ROW F: 1, 2, 4, 5, 10, 13, 14, 19, 20, 22, 23
ROW G: 3, 4, 5, 10, 11, 12, 13, 14, 19, 20, 21
ROW H: 3, 4, 5, 19, 20, 21
ROW I: 3, 4, 5, 19, 20, 21
ROW J: 1, 2, 4, 5, 6, 7, 8, 9, 10, 11, 12, 13, 14, 15, 16, 17, 18, 19, 20, 22, 23
ROW K: 4, 5, 8, 9, 10, 11, 12, 13, 14, 15, 16, 19, 20
ROW L: 4, 5, 7, 17, 19, 20
ROW M: 4, 5, 7, 17, 19, 20
ROW N: 4, 5, 7, 17, 19, 20,
ROW O: 4, 5, 7, 8, 9, 10, 11, 12, 13, 14, 15, 16, 17, 19, 20
ROW P: 4, 5, 6, 18, 19, 20
ROW Q: 5, 6, 7, 8, 9, 10, 11, 12, 13, 14, 15, 16, 17, 18, 19
ROW R: 10, 11, 12, 13, 14

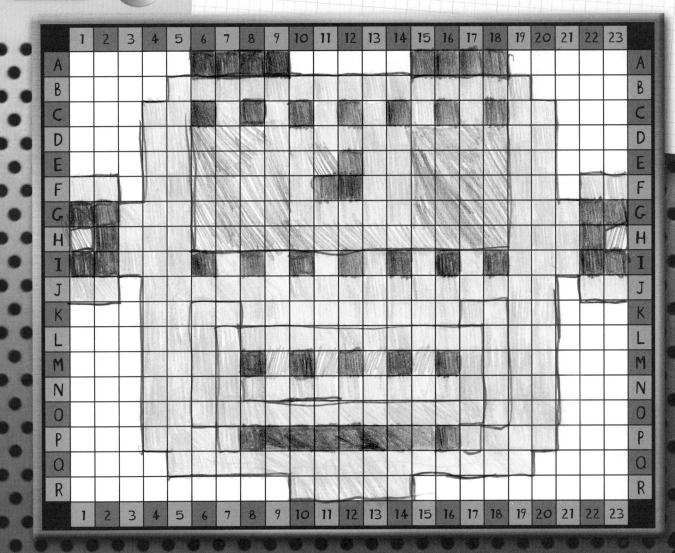

# CURSED CODE

Use the hieroglyphic code to decipher the dreaded curse of the mummy.

**THEN RUN!**

## FRIGHTFUL FACTS

WHEN THE TOMB OF THE PHARAOH TUTANKHAMEN WAS OPENED IN 1922 IT IS SAID THAT A CURSE WAS FOUND AT THE ENTRANCE. LORD CARNARVON, A WITNESS TO ITS DISCOVERY, DIED A FEW WEEKS LATER.

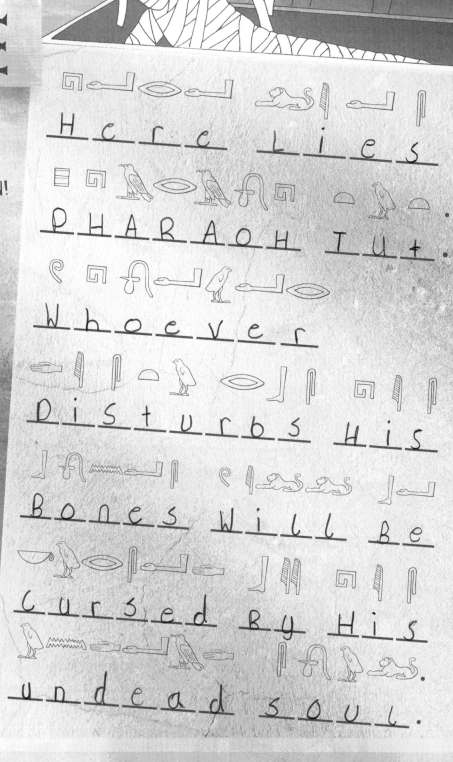

Here Lies
PHARAOH Tut.
Whoever
Disturbs His
Bones Will Be
Cursed By His
undead soul.

A B C D E F G H I J K L M

N O P Q R S T U V W X Y Z

The answer is at the back of the book.

# MONSTER MIRTH

Fill in the word balloons to make some hilarious Halloween jokes, then cackle like a crazy witch!

# Find the right home

Follow the lines to see where each dragon lives.

Answers are at the back of the book.

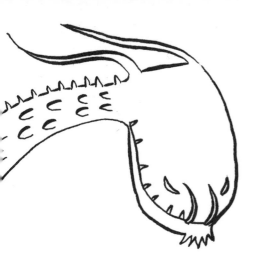

# Eye, eye

Which EYES will you draw on each dragon?

# Driving dot-to-dot

## 38 Who's taking a road trip down Route 66?

ROUTE 66 WAS A 3,940-KM ROAD THAT RAN ALL THE WAY FROM CHIGAGO TO LOS ANGELES IN THE USA.

Join up the dots to find out.

ROUTE US 66

# Jumping jigsaws

Everyone loves a bouncy castle on holiday.
Can you put this bouncy castle back together again?

Circle the jigsaw piece that is missing
from the picture.

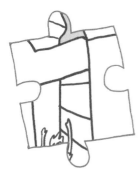   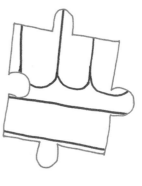

# Make me happy

Draw happy expressions on the dwarfs' faces. Snow White is alive!

# It's a-maze-ing!

The prince is taking Snow White back to his palace. Can you show them the way through the maze?

The answer is at the back of the book

# How to draw a pirate
## Copy each step-by-step drawing into the boxes below.

First, draw a circle for the head with a line going across the middle of it. Then draw a square body.

Draw two lines between the square and the circle for the neck. Add two arms and some trousers..

Good start!

Getting there!

Practise drawing some more pirates in a notebook!

Put a circle and triangle next to his head to make a hat. Now give your pirate hands and boots.

Finally, this pirate needs eyes, a mouth, a dagger, an eye patch, a belt, and spots on his hat.

Almost done!

Great work!

# Fabulous faces

Draw some lovely make-up on these girls.

dazzling

sophisticated

scary

natural

brightly coloured

44

# Model muddle

Unhappy about being the latest fashion accessories, these pets have tangled up their leads.

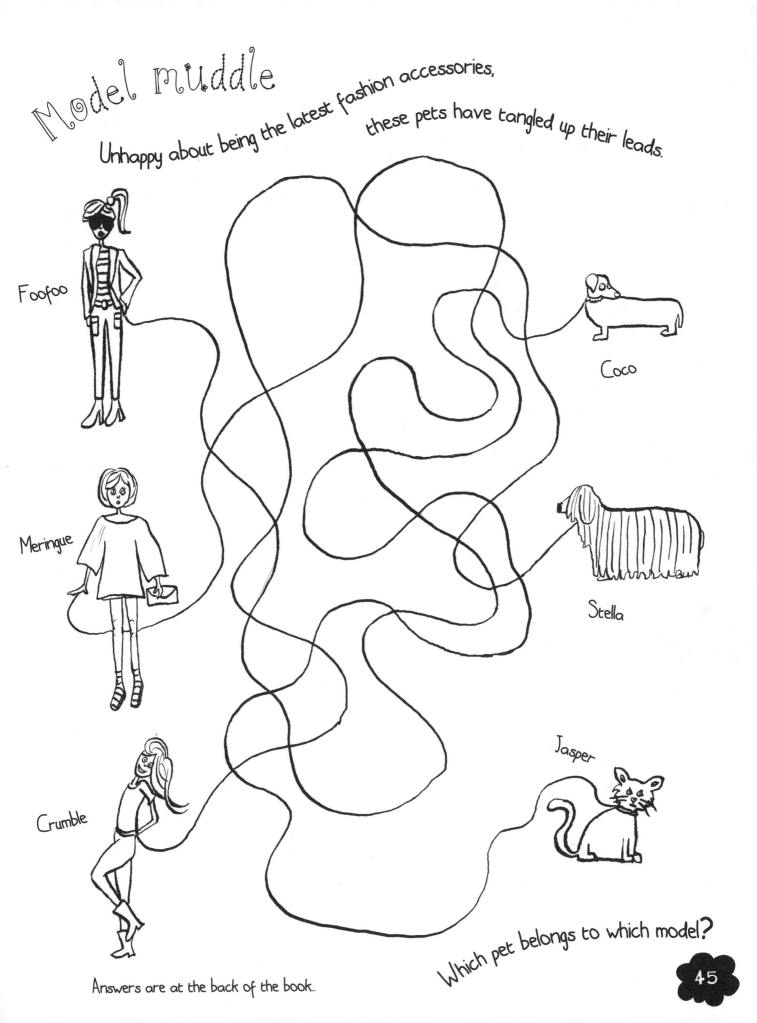

Foofoo

Coco

Meringue

Stella

Crumble

Jasper

Which pet belongs to which model?

Answers are at the back of the book..

# Loopy lines

Oops! These stage stars have got some of their lines wrong! Circle the mistakes below.

The answers are at the back of the book.

# Dance freeze

Play this game to find out who has the COOLEST dance moves.

Play one of your fave tunes to dance to!

FREEZE!

## HOW TO PLAY

- Take turns to be in charge of the music. Your friends should start dancing when the music begins.
- Let everyone dance for a bit, then stop the music and shout "FREEZE"!

- When the dancers hear "FREEZE" they must stop dancing. Anyone who moves is out.
- Continue playing until only one dancer is left - they are the winner and the COOLEST DANCER!

# ROCKET LAUNCH

To get up into space you'll need a rocket. Draw your own in this step-by-step guide.

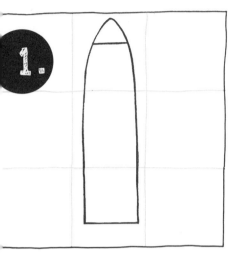

**1.** Draw the main body of your rocket with a cone at the top.

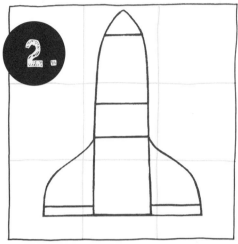

**2.** Add two lines halfway down the rocket and wings at the bottom.

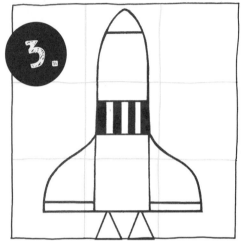

**3.** Draw two triangular thrusters at the bottom of the rocket. Add stripes to the middle section.

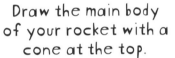

**4.** 3-2-1 blast-off! Draw flames and smoke coming from the engines.

**DID YOU KNOW?**
Your rocket will need to reach a speed of 7 miles per second to leave Earth. That speed would get you from London to New York in less than ten minutes!

# Count the dragons

How many dragons are in this egg? Colour them in.

Answer is at the back of the book.

# Who's knitting?

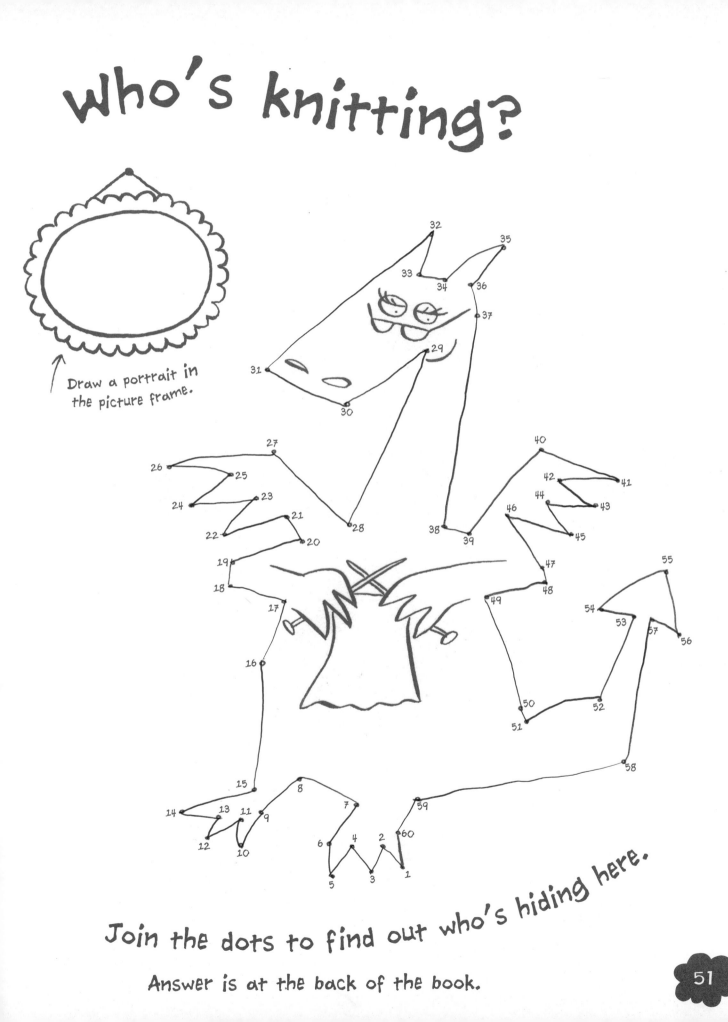

Draw a portrait in the picture frame.

Join the dots to find out who's hiding here.

Answer is at the back of the book.

51

# BATS ABOUT

Vampire bats are flitting through the moonlight in search of blood.

Look carefully at the silhouettes of the bats. Can you find **10** pairs and one extra? The bat left over is the one that wants to bite you!

The answer is at the back of the book.

## FRIGHTFUL FACTS

VAMPIRE BATS LIVE IN CENTRAL AND SOUTH AMERICA.
THEY FEED AT NIGHT, BITING A HOLE IN THE FLESH OF SLEEPING ANIMALS BEFORE LAPPING UP THEIR BLOOD. Slurp!

# MONSTER ON THE LOOSE!

**IT'S ESCAPED!** Design your own monster and show it breaking free from its cage.

You could give it tentacles, claws, fangs, hair, horns or spikes — go craaaaaazy!

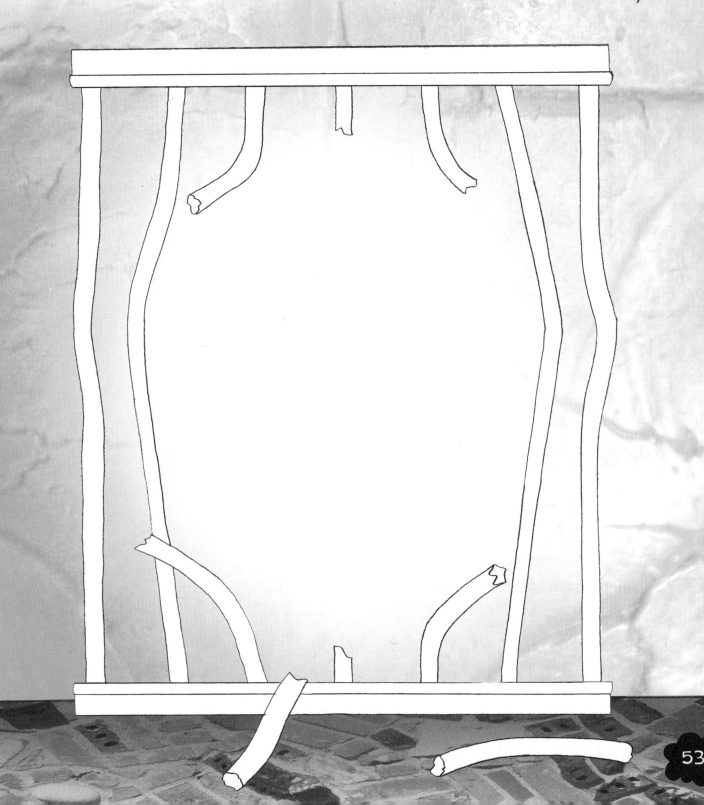

53

# old crone cosmetics
## Turn the queen into an old woman in four easy steps!

**1** From beautiful queen...

**2** to poor peasant woman...

1. Copy the image above.

2. Add a scarf and shawl.

to poor and ugly
peasant woman...

to poor and ugly
old crone!

3. Give her an open mouth
and scraggly hair.

4. Draw age lines
and black teeth!

# Message in a bottle

Some holiday destinations are so special, visitors try to keep them a secret!

This tourist has even written a message home in code. Use the letter key to help you decipher the message.

Message:

HGZBRMT LM Z IVNLGV YVZXS, UZI ZDZB UILN ZMBLMV. MVD AVZOZMW RH GSV YVHG!

A = Z
B = Y
C = X
D = W
E = V
F = U
G = T
H = S
I = R
J = Q
K = P
L = O
M = N
N = M
O = L
P = K
Q = J
R = I
S = H
T = G
U = F
V = E
W = D
X = C
Y = B
Z = A

Staying on a remote beach, far away from anyone. New zealand is the best!

The answer is at the back of the book.

# Cable car ride

These cable cars are working hard to climb the steep mountain slope.

Only one of the cars is different to the rest - can you spot the odd one out?

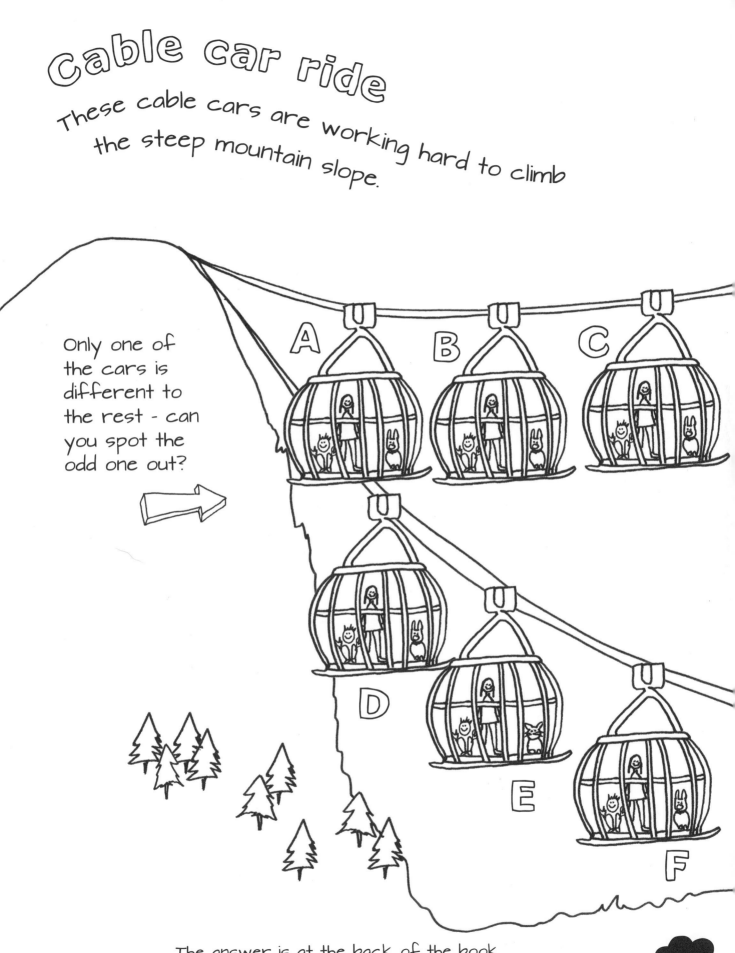

The answer is at the back of the book.

# Ship's stores

Fill the shelves with food, ready for a long sea voyage.

stinky cheese

beans    more beans

maggoty meat

# Top hats

Add some bows and buckles to these stylish hats then colour them in.

59

# Down at the salon...

Why not try something different with your hair?
(Ask a grown-up to help you if you get stuck.)

## How to plait your hair

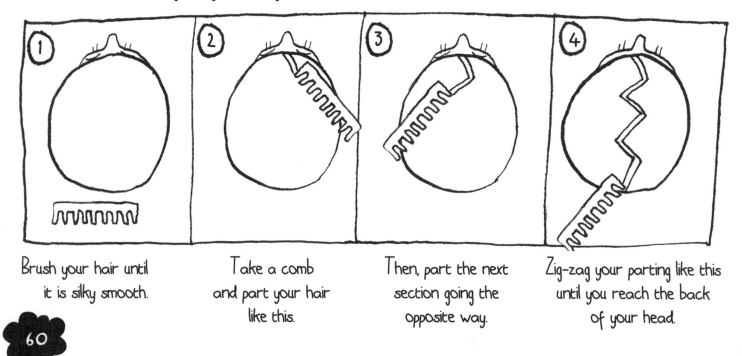

| 1 | 2 | 3 | 4 | 5 |
|---|---|---|---|---|
| Divide your hair into three strands. | Put the first strand over the second. | Then, put the third strand over the first | Next, put the second strand over the third. | Repeat these steps to the end, then secure with a tie. |

## How to make a zig-zag parting

| 1 | 2 | 3 | 4 |
|---|---|---|---|
| Brush your hair until it is silky smooth. | Take a comb and part your hair like this. | Then, part the next section going the opposite way. | Zig-zag your parting like this until you reach the back of your head. |

# That really suits you!

Draw a hairstyle for each of these characters.

princess

baby

actress

wizard

teenager

schoolboy

bride

goblin

61

# How to make your musical badges

1 Pull out this page and glue it to a thick piece of card.

2 Cut around the shapes to make your badges.

3 Stick safety pins to the backs with pieces of sticky tape.

4 Wear with attitude!

# Star turns

Play this great red-carpet role-play game with your mates.

63

## HOW TO PLAY

It's the big premiere. Give out the roles below and act out a red carpet scene. Swap roles so that everyone gets to be the star.

## MOVIE STAR

Dress up as a movie star. Pose for photos, sign autographs and answer questions.

## STAR REPORTER

Get an exclusive interview on the red carpet.

## FAN

You're their number-one fan! Get an autograph or a photo with your screen idol.

## PAPARAZZI

Pretend you've got a camera and get snapping!

Here are some questions for the reporter to ask:

- What's your name?
- Tell me about your latest movie.
- Which heartthrob actor would you like to work with?
- If you won an award, who would you dedicate it to?
- Who designed your fabulous outfit?

# SPACE LOG

Fill in the details of your space adventure in this journal, then add some drawings to go with it.

Ready for take-off! ...................................
..........................................................................................
..........................................................................................

..........................................................................................

Three days later we were on the Moon ...............
..........................................................................................
..........................................................................................
..........................................................................................
..........................................................................................

There was a lot happening at Mars base ...............
..........................................................................................
..........................................................................................
..........................................................................................

We were under attack!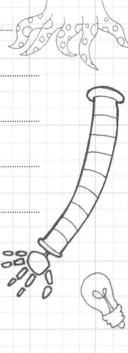

Our robot needed repairs

I got to meet my first alien, and new best friend

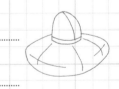

It was the furthest from Earth I have ever been

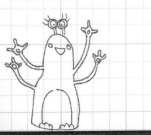
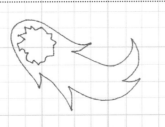

# Secret dragon map

Draw a magical dragon map using the pictures below.

little cottages

deserted castle

snowy mountains

dark caves

whistling woods

passing sheep

dragon hills

winding river

stepping stones

You could draw some hidden treasure!

# OUT-OF-SIGHT FRIGHT

Screaming Scarlett is running from an invisible monster.
She can hear it howling! Complete the dot-to-dot puzzle
to reveal the hidden ghoul.

The answer is at the
back of the book

# PREPARE TO SCARE!

WARNING! Only witches, wizards, vampires, ghosts or zombies are allowed past this point!

Take the Terrible Test below to proceed further.

- ◯ Do you like to stay up late?
- ◯ Do you like to bite people?
- ◯ Do your raggedy clothes stink?
- ◯ Do you like to creep up on people?
- ◯ Do you wish you could turn people into frogs?
- ◯ Do you hate cleaning your room?
- ◯ Do you have hairy hands and feet?

If you checked off one or more of the boxes, this book is for you.

Now turn the page, if you dare!

# Fairy-tale fashion

Design your own dresses for Snow White to wear.

1. Cut out the clothes on the back of the pretty paper on page 73.

2. Decide what you'd like Snow White to wear. Mix and match the different patterns.

3. Glue your outfit onto Snow White. Use ribbon or sequins to customize your design.

4. With the leftover paper you could try designing your own clothes for Snow White.

# Snow White's style

Stick your paper designs onto these
pictures of Snow White.

At home with
the dwarfs

At the palace

Trace these pictures onto
plain paper if you want
to design more outfits.

Cut out these clothes or design your own.

# Colourful characters

Here are a few of the most terrible pirates that have ever lived. Read about their fearsome ways and colour in their pictures.

## Sir Henry Morgan

This fancy dresser made many successful raids on passing ships. He was said to be very cruel and was also known as the Buccaneer King. Even though he was arrested he was eventually released and managed to die peacefully at home. Impressive!

## Blackbeard

Blackbeard (real name Edward Teach) was one of the most famous pirates of all. Tall, bearded, dark and terrifying, he would make himself even scarier by putting lighted matches under his hat during battles. He was finally shot at the age of 30, bringing his reign of terror to an end!

# Ching Shih

Ching Shih was one of the best pirates that ever lived. She took over as leader of the Red Flag Fleet when her pirate husband died. Her punishments were terrible and she destroyed over 60 Chinese naval ships. She died at the very old age (for a pirate) of 69!

# Captain Kidd

William Kidd started out as a pirate hunter. But instead of chasing them, Kidd decided to become a pirate himself! Sadly for him, he was captured and killed but it is said that he hid a lot of his treasure before being caught. Some of it was found, but many believe there is still some left to be discovered....

# Black Bart

This well-dressed fellow (real name Bartholomew Roberts), was captured by pirates as a young man. You might think this made him unhappy, but no! He soon grew to be one of the most successful pirates ever, capturing over 400 ships. He was finally shot and killed in a sea battle.

# Learn the lingo

Make up a brand-new language for these people to speak.

What name will you give your language and what country is it spoken in?

# Souvenir spend-up

You have €5.00 to buy presents for your friends back home.

€0.95

€0.50

€1.20

€2.00

€1.50

Can you afford all of the things on the shelves?

Total = _____

The answers are the end of the book

# Showtime!

This band needs to get dressed in a hurry.
Draw the girls some cool stage outfits.

Marissa M.
sings sweetly.

Baby Hoop
likes her bling!

Dress the band by drawing in their outfits.

Backflip Bella
has a sporty style.

JJ Jump
is street cool.

# Born to ✿✿✿✿✿?

Join the dots to find out what this girl is doing.

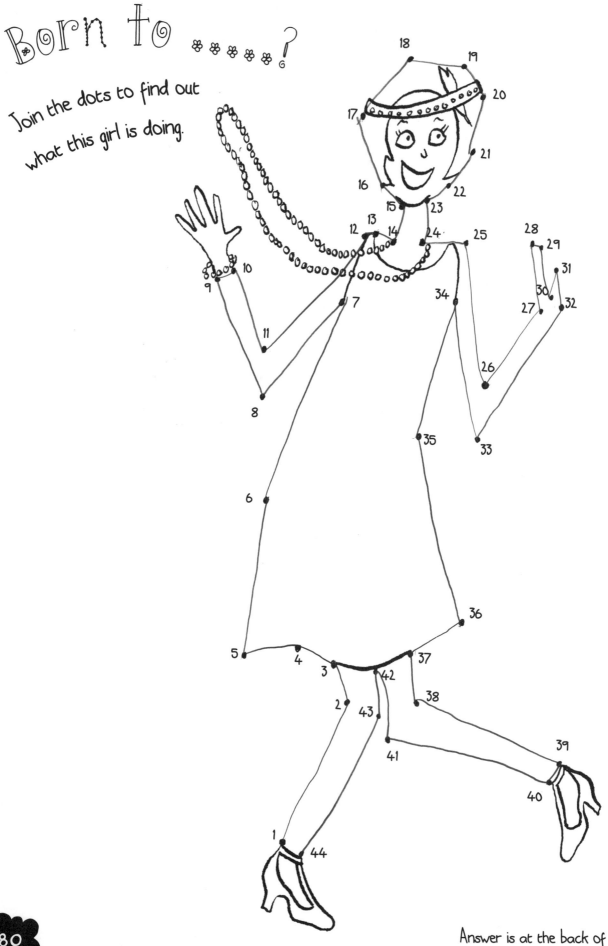

Answer is at the back of the book.

# On the catwalk

Read the descriptions, then draw the models in the spotlights below.

Persephone looks fabulous in this magenta mini-skirt with contrasting tangerine top. Set to be one of this season's MUST-HAVES.

January is UTTERLY GORGEOUS in this apricot bikini with matching picnic basket. The use of foil is striking.

Pomegranate's flaming red hair sets off this velvet romper suit perfectly. The pink wellies are an AWESOME addition.

Are those pyjamas or daywear? Who cares! The pretty flowers look so delicate against Zoë's pale skin. WOW!

# ROCKET PLAQUE

Make your own shiny plaque to commemorate your space adventure.

**WHAT YOU NEED**
Pencil
Scissors
Cardboard
Card
Aluminium foil
Black paint and brush

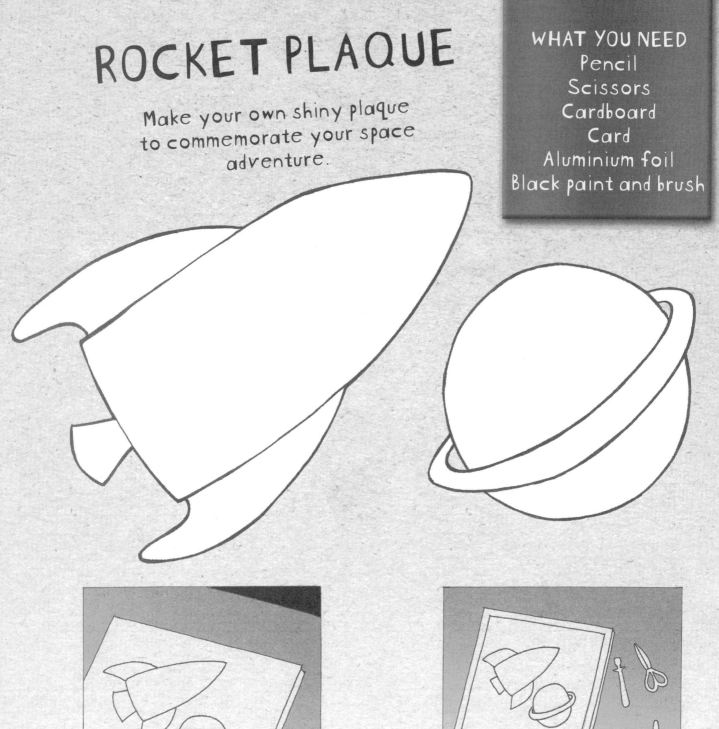

**1.** Copy the outline of the spaceship and planet onto cardboard.

**2.** Cut them out and stick them onto a new square of card. Add a cardboard frame.

**3.** Glue foil over the top of the whole picture and rub it down to show the shapes underneath.

**4.** Use black paint to fill in the space between the shapes and frame. Let it dry, then hang it up in your bedroom!

83

# HOW TO DRAW A SCARY FACE

Copy each step to draw your own scary face.

You can use it to decorate Halloween cards or party invites.

**1.** Draw an oval with two large, round eyeholes.

**2.** Sketch two slits for the nostrils and a wide, open mouth.

**3.** Add teeth in the mouth, a crack on the head, and two curves either side of the eyes.

**4.** Finish by drawing a pair of googly eyes and fill in the mouth and eyeholes with black.

## FRIGHTFUL FACT

TWO THOUSAND YEARS AGO IN MONGOLIA, IT WAS THE TRADITION FOR BARBARIAN WARRIORS TO USE THE SKULLS OF THEIR SLAIN ENEMIES AS DRINKING CUPS.

# WITCH STYLE

Wynona the Witch is going to a Halloween party!

Use the colour code to help her glam up her outfit for the big night.

1 ✸ Black
2 ✸ Green
3 ✸ Skin colour
4 ✸ Purple
5 ✸ Pink
6 ✸ Yellow
7 ✸ Brown

# How to draw a dragon

First, draw the dragon's BODY.
It looks a bit like a thumb.

Next, add a long SNOUT,
sharp SPIKES and a beady EYE.

Good start!

Getting there!

# Copy each of the drawing steps into the boxes below.

Now, make it breathe FIRE and add a menacing MOUTH and monstrous FEET.

Finally, give it WINGS on its back and a terrible TAIL.

Almost done!

Great work!

# The royal family album

Can you complete the eight pictures of Snow White as she grows up from baby to bride?

Baby

Crawling

Toddler

Skipping child

Teenager

The fairest of them all!

The runaway

Happy bride

89

# Pirate Pete's parrot

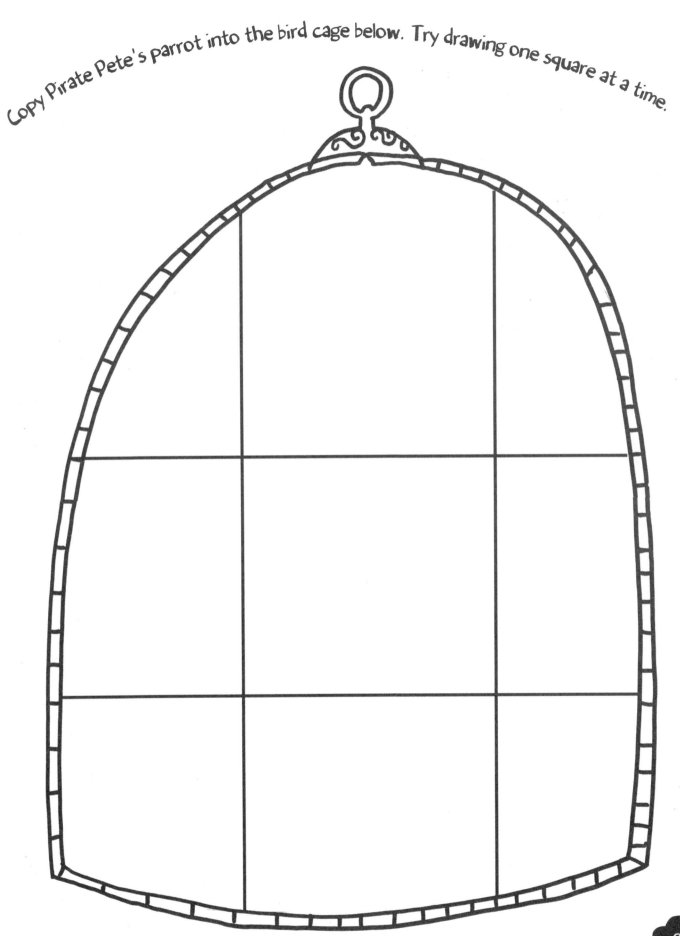

91

# House exchange

## Try something different this year and organize a house exchange!

If you could swap houses for a fortnight with a family from another country, what kind of home would you choose? Colour them all in!

Native American tepee

Inuit igloo

Kenyan tribal hut

Swiss chalet

Japanese pagoda

# Funny food

## What will you eat on holiday?

Add some delicious toppings to this pizza. Can you draw the ingredients in a pattern that makes you smile?

PIZZAS HAVE BEEN EATEN FOR THOUSANDS OF YEARS! EVEN THE ANCIENT GREEKS LIKED TO EAT FLATBREADS TOPPED WITH HERBS, ONION AND GARLIC.

My favourite pizza topping is
_____

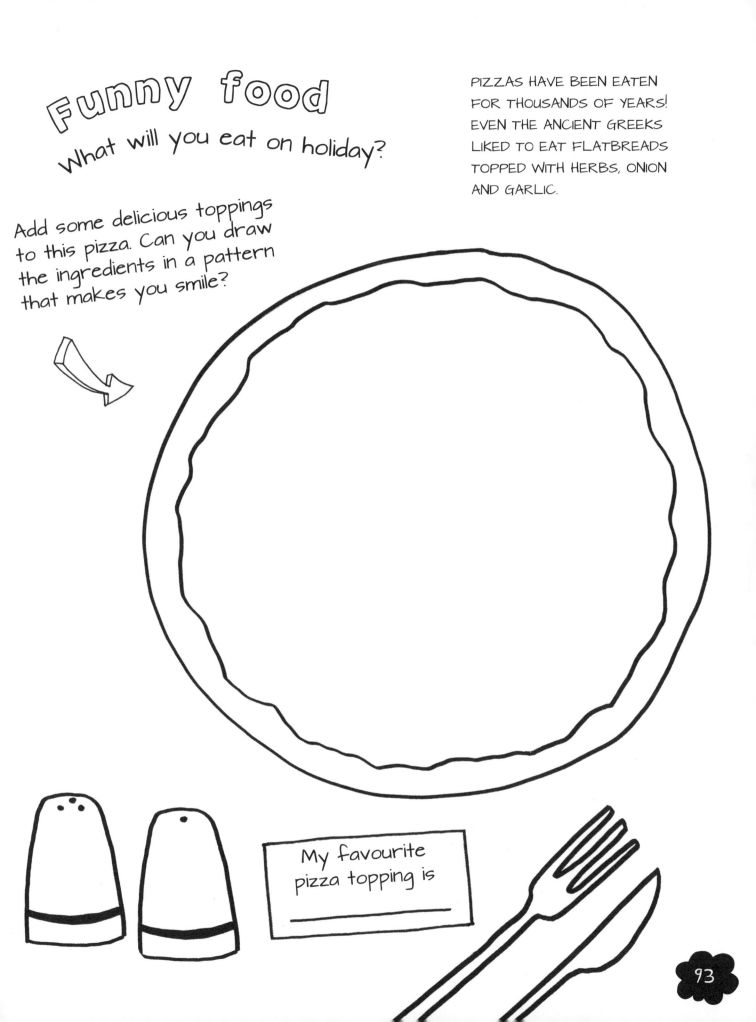

# Fan mail messages

This page is for your fans. Ask them to write special messages for you.

Start with your BFFs (Best Fans Forever)!

# A star is born

Fill your dressing table with all the things you need to get a superstar look.

95

# Design workshop

Draw some gorgeous patterns
on this year's hot swimwear.

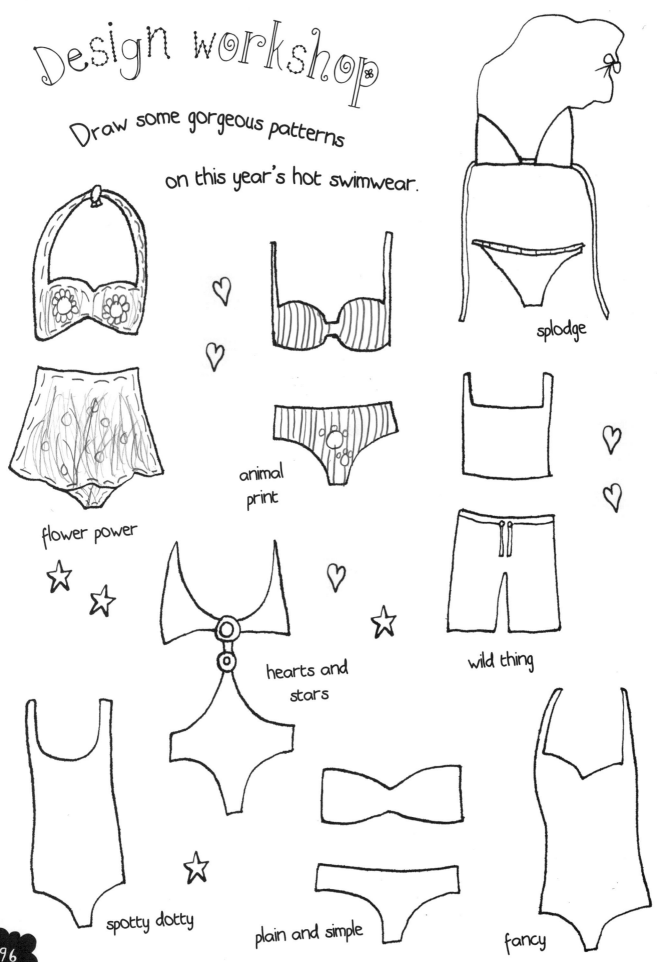

splodge

flower power

animal print

hearts and stars

wild thing

spotty dotty

plain and simple

fancy

# A long time ago...
...this dress was the latest fashion!

Draw in the other half of this lady.

# STARGAZER

For thousands of years people have found their way across the sky by giving names to groups of stars called constellations. Here are just a few.

## PERSEUS
Perseus defeated the monstrous snake-headed Medusa whose stare turned people to stone. He carries her head in one hand and a sword in the other.

## AURIGA
Legend says that Auriga invented the chariot. He rides it across the night sky, carrying a young goat under his arm.

## CASSIOPEIA
Cassiopeia was a queen who got in trouble with the gods for boasting that she was one of the most beautiful women in the world.

## ORION
Orion, the son of the sea god Poseidon, was a great hunter but a bit of a bighead. Despite all his fighting skills, he was killed by a tiny scorpion.

## TAURUS
Taurus the bull is one of the 12 signs of the zodiac in the night sky. In Greek myth, the king of the gods, Zeus, disguised himself as a bull.

When you're travelling in outer space, you'll see different stars to the ones that are visible from Earth.

Draw some of the new constellations that you think you might find.

# PERFECT PUMPKINS

Here's how to design the perfect jack-o'-lantern.

Draw these pictures onto your hollowed-out pumpkin, then ask a grown-up to carefully cut out the shapes. Put a candle inside to light up the lantern's fearsome features.

## Funky face

Use crescent moons for eyebrows, small circles for the eyes, and draw a goofy, toothy smile.

## Starry sky

Use the star stencil to draw lots of stars on your pumpkin for a stellar surprise.

## Fangs a lot!

Draw triangular eyes and a wide, fanged grin for a vampire visage.

## Bloodcurdling bat

Copy a bat shape on both sides of your pumpkin.

## FRIGHTFUL FACTS

ORIGINALLY JACK-O'-LANTERN WAS THE NAME GIVEN TO A FLAMING SPIRIT THAT INHABITED SWAMPY MARSHLANDS. THE SPIRIT WOULD LEAD LOST TRAVELLERS TO THEIR DOOM IN THE DEEP BOGS.

# SLURPY SOUP

Pumpkins are not just for carving.

Here's a recipe for a delicious pumpkin soup that you can serve using the pumpkin as the bowl!

## ✤ INGREDIENTS ✤

Medium pumpkin ⚡ 1 onion, peeled ◉ 1 tablespoon olive oil

2 teaspoons cumin ◎ 4 cups warm vegetable stock

1 tablespoon natural yogurt

## ✤ STEPS ✤

1. Cut away the top of the pumpkin.

2. Scoop out the seeds and stringy bits inside and discard them.

3. Using a spoon, dig out the pumpkin flesh, being careful not to break through the sides of the pumpkin.

4. Chop the onion and fry it in the oil in a large pan for about five minutes.

5. Stir in the cumin, then add the chopped pumpkin flesh and stir it with the onions for about 10 minutes.

6. Pour in the warm stock and leave to simmer for 15 minutes until the pumpkin is soft.

7. Let the mixture cool a little before asking a grown-up to help you blend it into a soup. Pour the soup into the pumpkin shell and serve it to your Halloween guests with a ladle. Add a swirl of yogurt to each bowl.

# The dragon and me

I was lying in bed when suddenly I heard a noise. I opened the curtains and peered out. Good Lord! A fire-breathing dragon! "Hop on my back," it said. "I'm taking you for a ride."

I climbed aboard and as I looked down, I could see

... a cat and a bat,

... an elegant owl,

... a thief in the night

... and a fox on the prowl.

Draw in all the things the little boy could see.

# Book of spells

## Make up a spell to turn someone ugly!

Ingredients:

Two drops of _Poison_

A pinch of _Musty Crusty Toenails_

The ground-up tooth of a _Mummy, (not your mummy!)_

Nose hairs from a _Baboon_

Spit from a _Frog_

To cast the spell, say these words:

_Musty dusty Crusty 123!_

Make up a spell
to turn sprouts
into sweets!

Ingredients:

A bag of smelly sprouts
A cup of Milk
A spoonful of Sugar
A ripe Watermelon
A Lillac flower
The Fluff from a teddy

To cast the spell, say these words:

Cutie tootie tchehe!

# Fabulous frocks

Colour in these movie premiere dresses.

# The hottest hair in town

These pop stars are visiting Bouffant Barnets.

Give them crazy hairstyles that will look great on stage.

# And the award goes to...

Cross out the lines you wouldn't say in your acceptance speech.

Thank you for this amazing award.

I couldn't care less about this award.

My director was rubbish. I would never work with him/her again.

I'd like to thank my co-star Amanda. She's my new best friend.

This was the most fun film I've ever worked on.

Thank you to everyone who believed in me.

I hope I never make another film with cats and dogs.

I'm donating all my money to an animal sanctuary.

Maybe it wasn't such a good idea to collect this award in my pyjamas!

# Baggage carousel

A busy flight has just landed!

Count the pieces of luggage piled up on the baggage carousel, then colour it in.

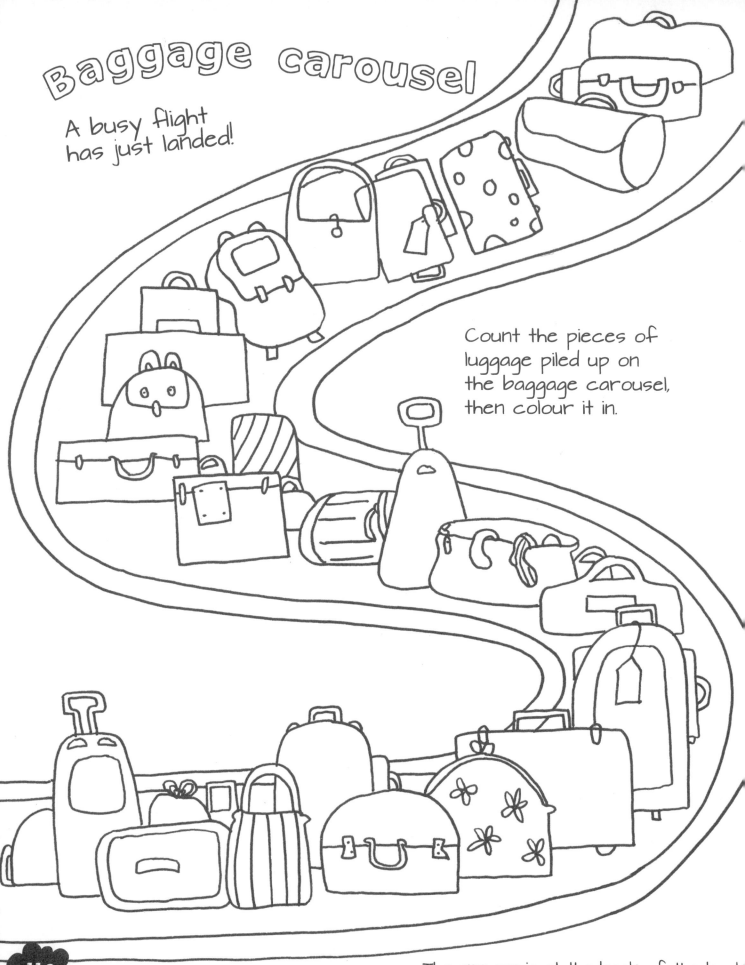

The answer is at the back of the book

# Mad menus

Some of the meals on this menu are rather exotic!

Take the tick test to decide which ones are genuine dishes from around the world and which ones are false.

## NAUGHTY NOSH RESTAURANT

1. Bird's nest soup
   - ☐ True
   - ☐ False

2. Armadillo pie
   - ☐ True
   - ☐ False

3. Fried tarantulas
   - ☐ True
   - ☐ False

4. Snake wine
   - ☐ True
   - ☐ False

5. Meerkat munchies
   - ☐ True
   - ☐ False

6. Reindeer steaks
   - ☐ True
   - ☐ False

The answers are at the back of the book.

# Fashion doodles...

Pretend to be a top fashion designer and create some lovely designs on this special drawing paper.

# Keeping cool

Draw some pretty patterns on these fans, then colour them in.

How to make a fabulous fan

Draw a pattern on one side of some paper, then fold it back and forth.

Open the paper out and glue a lolly stick to each end.

Refold it and fasten the end of the sticks together.

# DON'T LOSE YOUR HEAD!

The Headless Horror is here to haunt you.

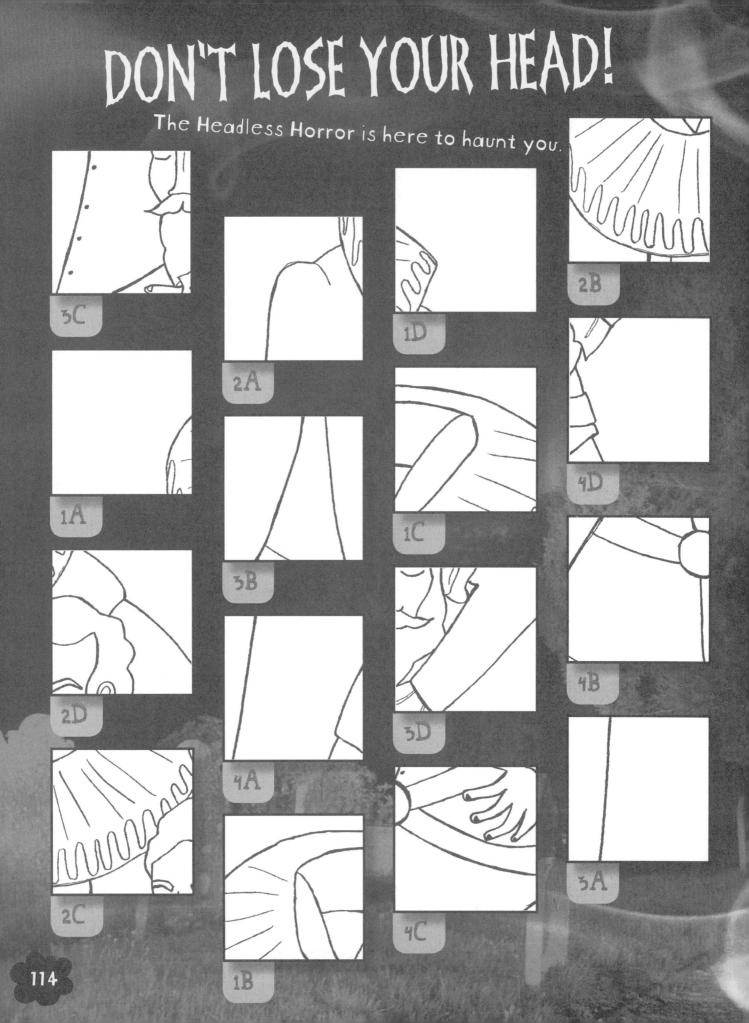

Copy the picture, square by square,
in the correct order into the grid below
to see him in his full grisly glory.

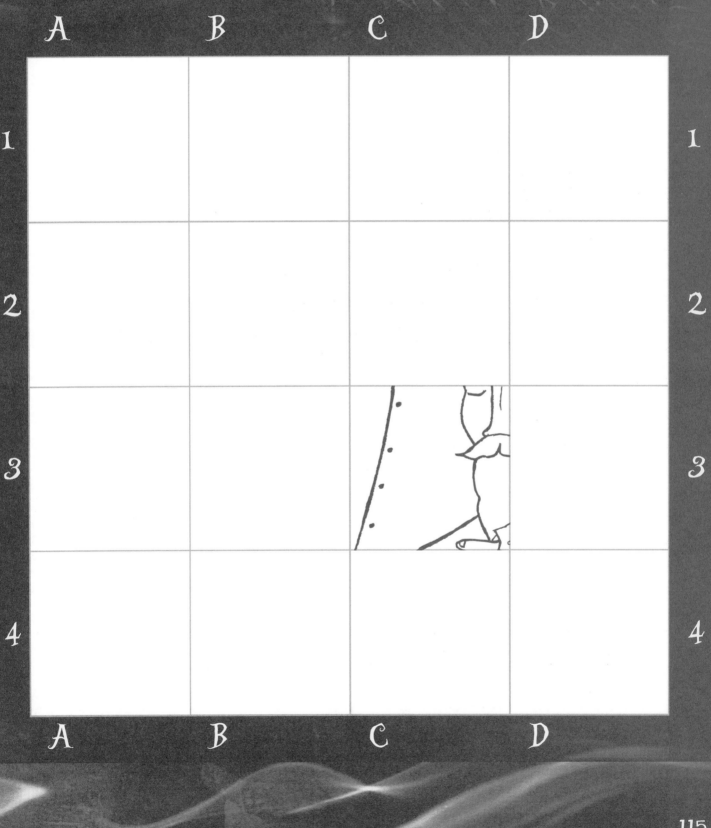

# GALAXY GAZETTE

Draw yourself here.

Read all about the galaxy's top stories and draw pictures to go with them.

## ALIEN PET EATS OWNER

Mrs Jean Ritter of Leeds did not read the warning that came with her pet carnipod and tried to feed it cat food.

## SATURN STAR

The solar system's youngest astronaut has now reached Saturn.

## METEOR DANGER!

Astronomers say a one-mile -wide meteor will pass very close to Earth next week. Let's hope it misses us!

## CAN WE HAVE OUR BALL BACK?

The Mars vs Moon football final was cancelled yesterday when the ball was kicked out of orbit.

# METEORITE BITES

Bake these mouth-watering space snacks
to share with your starship crew.

## INGREDIENTS

225g self-raising flour

1 tsp baking powder

110g butter

55g brown sugar

1 tsp mixed spice

160g mixed dried fruit
and raisins

1 egg

1 tbsp milk

icing sugar

## DIRECTIONS

**1.** In a bowl, mix together the flour, baking powder and butter until it's crumbly. Then add the sugar, spice and dried fruit.

**2.** Beat the egg in a cup, then stir it into the mix, with the milk, to make a soft dough.

**3.** Scoop out tablespoons of the mix, mould them into lumpy meteorite shapes and place them on a baking tray.

**4.** Sprinkle a little icing sugar on top for stardust, then ask a grown-up to bake them in an oven at 200°C for 15 minutes until golden. Leave them to cool before eating.

# A crown fit for a princess

Here's how to make your crown.

**1.** Carefully cut out the two sides of the crown.

**2.** Colour in the jewels.

**3.** Use sticky tape to join tabs A and B, and tabs C and D.

**4.** You can stick matching jewels onto your ears to complete your regal look!

**5.** Practise your royal wave and ask your family to curtsey or bow whenever you walk into the room!

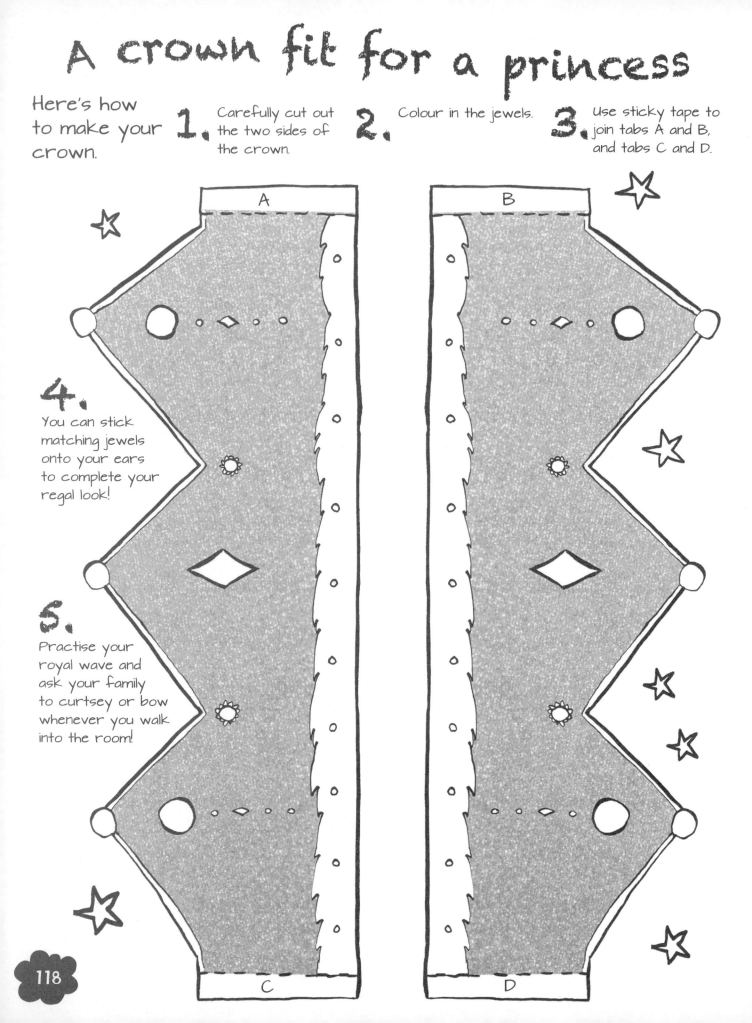

A

B

C

D

# Be Snow White's hair stylist

An up-do?

A down-do?

Elegant?

A wild and crazy hair-do?

Drop-dead gorgeous!

Natural?

You can add flowers, tiaras or anything you like!

# The Jolly Roger

A pirate flag is called a Jolly Roger. Pirates fly them to frighten other ships. Colour in these real Jolly Rogers, then make up one of your own.

The most famous JOLLY ROGER is the skull and crossbones. This pirate has added a scarf to his skull but it still looks scary!

Here is another skull and crossbones with the skull facing sideways. Whichever way the skull faces, it always means DEATH!

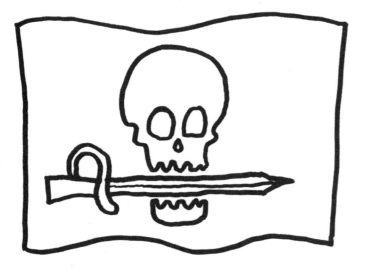

Pirates use SWORDS and DAGGERS to show they are powerful. This flag means power to the pirates and death to their enemies.

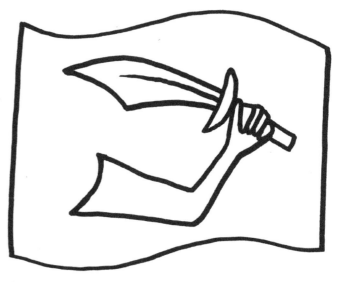

This flag belonged to the pirate THOMAS TEW. He was eventually killed by a sword like the one shown on his flag.

# Design your own pirate flag

Now draw and colour in your own Jolly Roger.

# It's mine, all mine

Colour in the DRAGON and its treasure.

# A-mazing

Help the knight find his way through the MAZE without waking the sleeping dragon. Shh!

START

THE END

The answer is at the back of the book.

# Celebrity closet

## What's in your wardrobe?

Pretty princess or cool rock chick? Draw in some stage outfits below.

HATS

SCARVES

BAGS

SHOES

SHOES

# Act the part

Good actors can turn themselves into a totally different character.

What you need:
• talcum powder
• grey or brown eye pencil
• shawl or blanket
• walking stick

Follow the steps to transform yourself into a little old lady.

1 First take the eye pencil and draw lines and wrinkles on your face.

2 Then tie your hair back in a bun, or brush it back if it is quite short.

3 Pat talcum powder all over your hair. This will turn it grey and make you look older.

4 Finally, wrap yourself in a shawl.

**TOP TIP**
PRACTISE WALKING LIKE AN ELDERLY PERSON - SLOWLY DOES IT. BEND YOUR KNEES AND HUNCH YOUR SHOULDERS.

125

# Pampered pet

Copy this sausage dog into the empty frame below. Try drawing one square at a time.

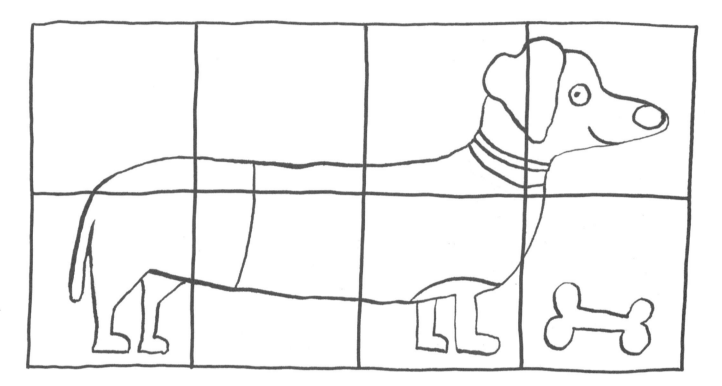

Give him a lovely patterned coat as well.

Call me!

Design a fabulous new
range of mobile-phone cases.

Leave some text
messages
on them too.

Holiday things to colour in

128

# Safari sketches

Lucky you! You're on an amazing safari trip in Africa.

What can you see through your binoculars today?

AFRICA'S BIG FIVE ANIMALS FOR SAFARI SPOTTERS.
1. LION
2. LEOPARD
3. RHINO
4. ELEPHANT
5. BUFFALO

BUT DON'T FORGET ABOUT GIRAFFES, HIPPOS AND GORILLAS, TOO!

# MAGIC POTIONS

Here's a pair of frightful fruity juices to share with your wizard and witch pals next time they come over for a spell.

## PURPLE OOZE

INGREDIENTS:
2 cups natural yogurt
1 cup blueberries
1 peeled banana
½ cup orange juice
Fake fly or bug

Ask a grown-up to mix all the ingredients in a blender until they form a thick, gooey mix that can be poured into two glasses. Decorate with a fake fly or bug (not to be swallowed!).

Add a straw.

## GREEN GOO

INGREDIENTS:
Lime-flavoured syrup
Apple juice
Lemonade
Handful of green grapes, cut into halves
Gummy worms

Pour 2cm of lime syrup into a tall glass, then add apple juice until it is half full.

Top it off with lemonade and sprinkle grape halves on top. Drape a gummy worm over the side of the glass.

# HAIRY HORROR

It's full moon!

Turn poor Johnny Lupus into a werewolf by drawing on a wolf's ears, claws, frightening fangs and lots of shaggy hair all over his body.

## FRIGHTFUL FACTS

HUNGARIAN LEGENDS TELL THAT WEREWOLVES LIVED IN AN AREA CALLED TRANSDANUBIA. YOUNG CHILDREN WHO RAN AWAY FROM HOME GAINED THE ABILITY TO CHANGE INTO FEARSOME WEREWOLVES THAT HUNTED AND FED ON WILD ANIMALS AT NIGHT.

# DESIGN A SPACE PROBE

Can you build your own space probe for studying the stars? Use the parts suggested, if you like, then launch it into space!

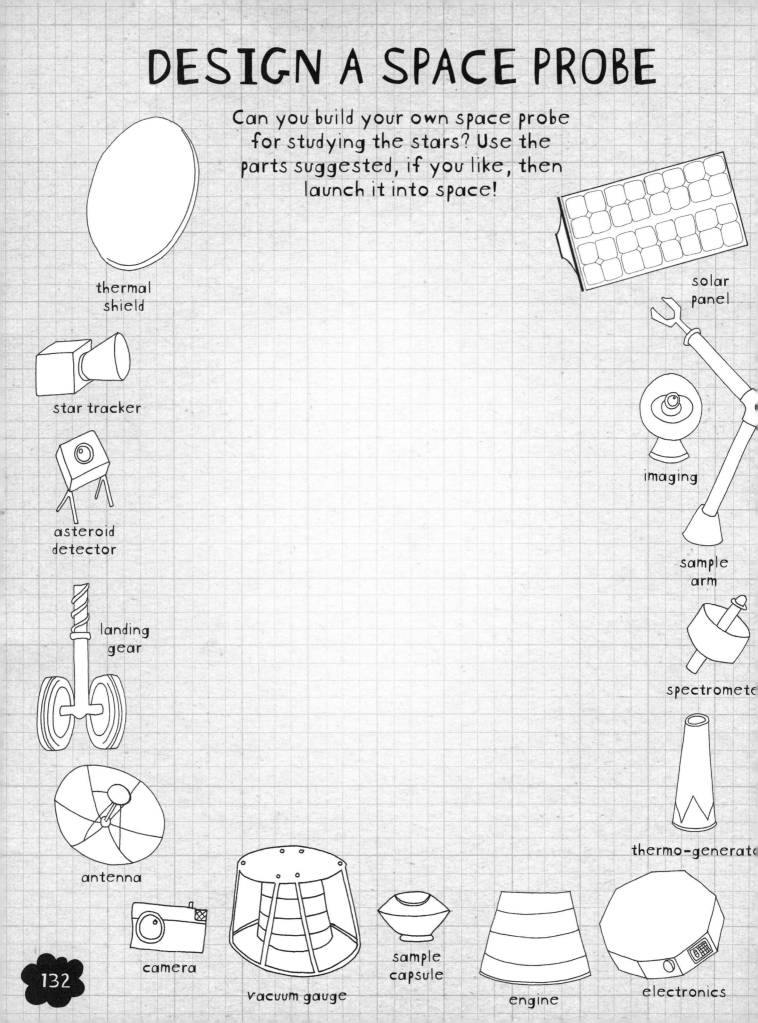

thermal shield

solar panel

star tracker

imaging

asteroid detector

sample arm

spectrometer

landing gear

antenna

thermo-generator

camera

vacuum gauge

sample capsule

engine

electronics

# TRUE OR FALSE?

**ASTEROID**
A rock, smaller than a planet, that orbits the Sun. Most asteroids are found between Mars and Jupiter.

True ⬤    False ⬤

**BLACK HOLE**
An area of space where gravity is so strong even light can't escape its pull.

True ⬤    False ⬤

**COMET**
An icy object travelling through space, leaving a trail of gas and dust behind it.

True ⬤    False ⬤

**GALAXY**
A collection of billions of stars, planets, dust and gas.

True ⬤    False ⬤

**GIBBULON**
A giant space monkey at the centre of our galaxy.

True ⬤    False ⬤

**LIGHT-YEAR**
The distance that light travels through space in one year – 5,878 billion miles.

True ⬤    False ⬤

**MILKY WAY**
The name of our galaxy.

True ⬤    False ⬤

**MOON**
A world that orbits a planet, such as Earth's Moon.

True ⬤    False ⬤

**OBLONGON**
A rectangular planet that orbits the Sun once every five minutes.

True ⬤    False ⬤

**SOLAR SYSTEM**
A star and the planets and objects that move around it.

True ⬤    False ⬤

**STAR**
A large ball of super-heated gas in space. The Sun is our nearest star.

True ⬤    False ⬤

**SUPERNOVA**
An exploding star.

True ⬤    False ⬤

**VORPAL DRIVE**
An experimental rocket engine that uses brainwaves to travel through space.

True ⬤    False ⬤

# Make up a fairy tale
Circle the pictures and fill in the gaps to make up your own story.

Once upon a time, a queen pricked her finger on a ......................................

needle    rose    hedgehog

She made a wish that she would have a little girl
and her name would be ......................................

Ruby    Amber    Violet

But the queen died and the king married again. The new queen
was evil. She hated her step-daughter and envied her beauty,
so she asked a huntsman to take her into the woods and
kill her, bringing back her ......................................

heart    shoes    mobile phone

The huntsman let the princess go, and she ran to a little house.
She was so tired she fell asleep on one of seven little beds.
She woke up to find seven ......................................

dwarfs    fairies    aliens

They had been digging for ......................................

precious gems    oil    dinosaur bones

They lived happily together until one day there was a knock
at the door and there stood a/an ......................................

old woman    snowman    elephant

Who gave the girl a poisoned ......................................

apple    lollipop    peanut butter sandwich

Luckily along came a ......................................

prince    frog    postman

Who gave her a ......................................

kiss    ring    some money

And ......................................
..........................................................................................
.......................................................................................... (Finish the story yourself!)

134

# A dream home
Join the dots to see where Snow White grew up.

The answer is
at the back of
the book

# Dragon-taming potions

What's inside the jars?
Draw in some of your own too.

# Pirate wars

### Who will be the first pirate to find all the treasure?

**1** CUT out the maps along the dotted lines on the following pages then find a pirate to play against!

**2** Take one map each and HIDE six lots of treasure on it. Use an X to mark each spot. Don't let the other player see.

**3** Take it in turns to CALL OUT a square (for example, E4). If you are not the caller, shout out FOUND or MISSED. The caller then marks F for found or M for missed in the right square.

**4** The first pirate to find all the other pirate's treasure is THE WINNER!

**5** Turn your paper over to play PIRATE WARS again! Make sure you both use the same map each time.

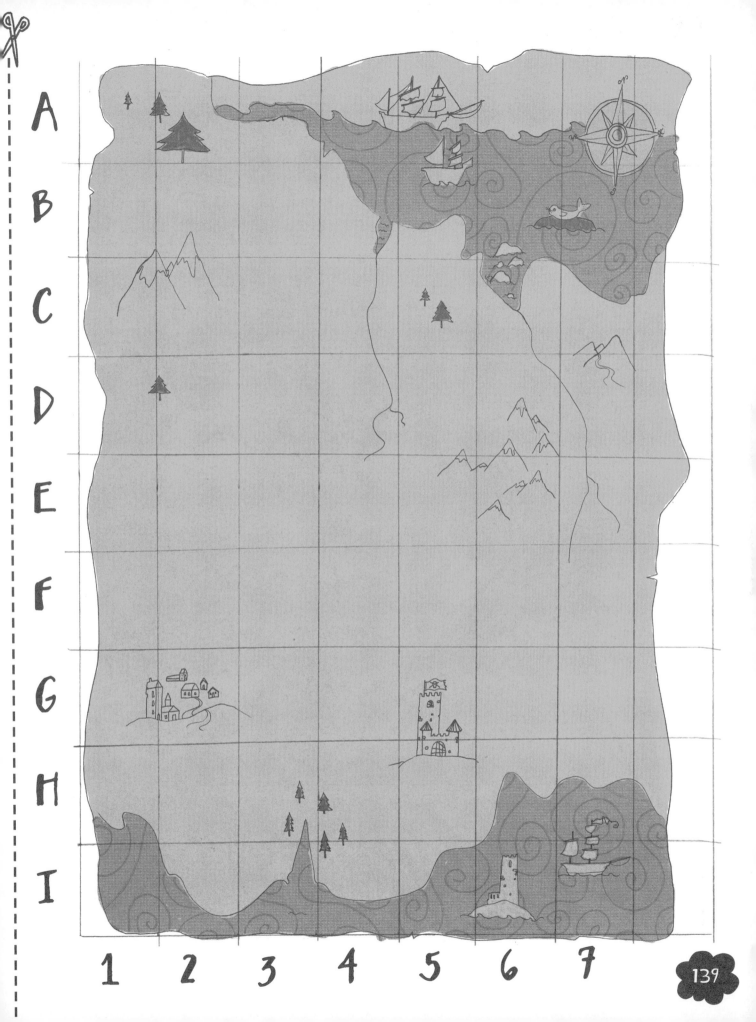

A B C D E F G H I

1 2 3 4 5 6 7

# Pretty Pollies

Put some colour back into these parrots.

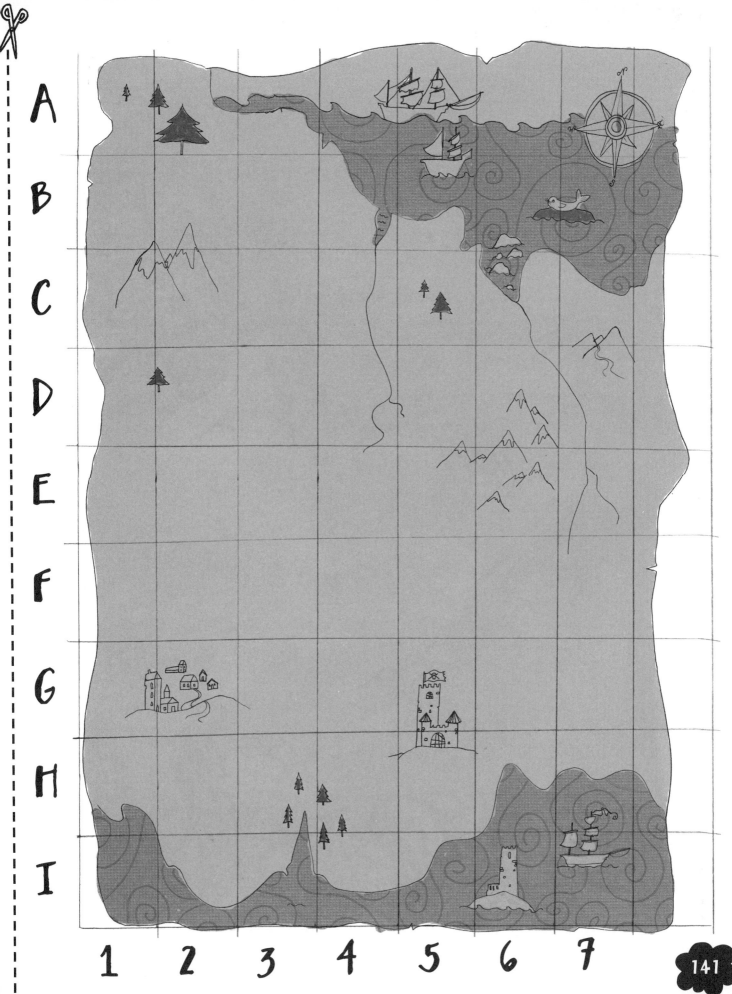

A
B
C
D
E
F
G
H
I

1 2 3 4 5 6 7

# MONSTER MASH

Igor has collected these body parts from the graveyard!

Copy them to build your own Frankenstein's monster,
then bring him to life with colour. And don't forget to add
some sinister stitches and bolts to hold him together!

# TALE OF TERROR

Make up your own ghost story.

There are gaps in this spine-chilling tale for you to add names, places and your scariest ideas.

Once it's finished, share it with a friend... late at night.

LATE ON HALLOWEEN NIGHT, a mist descended on _____. (Your name here) was soon lost and reached a dead end at an old iron gate. The gate was rusty and covered in _____, as if it had not been opened for centuries. Tired and hungry, (Your name here) pushed a way through and walked up to the house to ask directions.

The house looked _____. (Your name here) glimpsed a _____ moving past an upstairs window and felt a chill. There was a _____ sound from within and footsteps. (Your name here) stepped back and was grabbed by the ankle. It was a _____ reaching from the muddy ground. Then, the door opened and there stood _____ wearing _____. It spoke in a voice from beyond the grave and said "_____ _____." (Your name here) struggled to get free, but it was too late. The monster leaped forward and _____. That was the last that anyone ever heard of (Your name here).

 THE GRISLY END

# All in a day's work

Complete the outfits of these two busy people.

cute ponytail

impressive shoes

AIR STEWARDESS

TENNIS CHAMPION

# Pretty things

Colour in this beautiful jewellery

# Face-painting fun

At a day out at the fair these children are waiting to have their faces painted.

Find some bright colours then give each one a crazy new look!

Why not paint an animal face?

# Catch a coach

It's time to take a coach tour across France!

Study the coach timetable, then answer the questions at the bottom of the page.

| Timetable | Coach 1 | Coach 2 | Coach 3 | Coach 4 |
|---|---|---|---|---|
| Paris | 07:14 | 09:03 | 10:50 | 12:35 |
| Orléans | 09:24 | 11:13 | 13:00 | 14:45 |
| Bordeaux | 14:45 | 16:34 | | 20:06 |

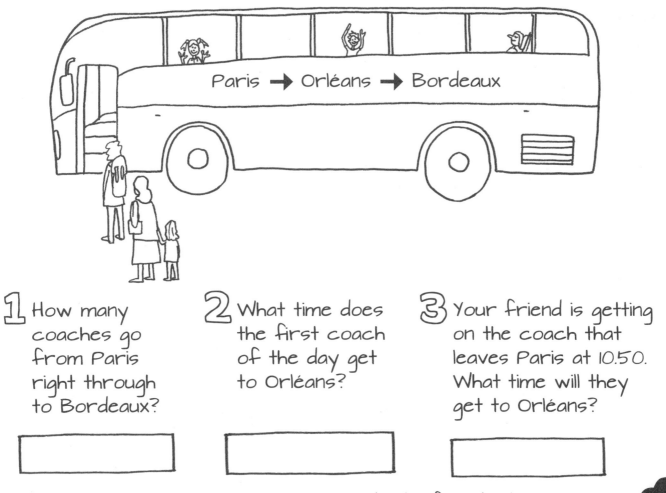

Paris → Orléans → Bordeaux

1 How many coaches go from Paris right through to Bordeaux?

2 What time does the first coach of the day get to Orléans?

3 Your friend is getting on the coach that leaves Paris at 10.50. What time will they get to Orléans?

The answers are at the back of the book.

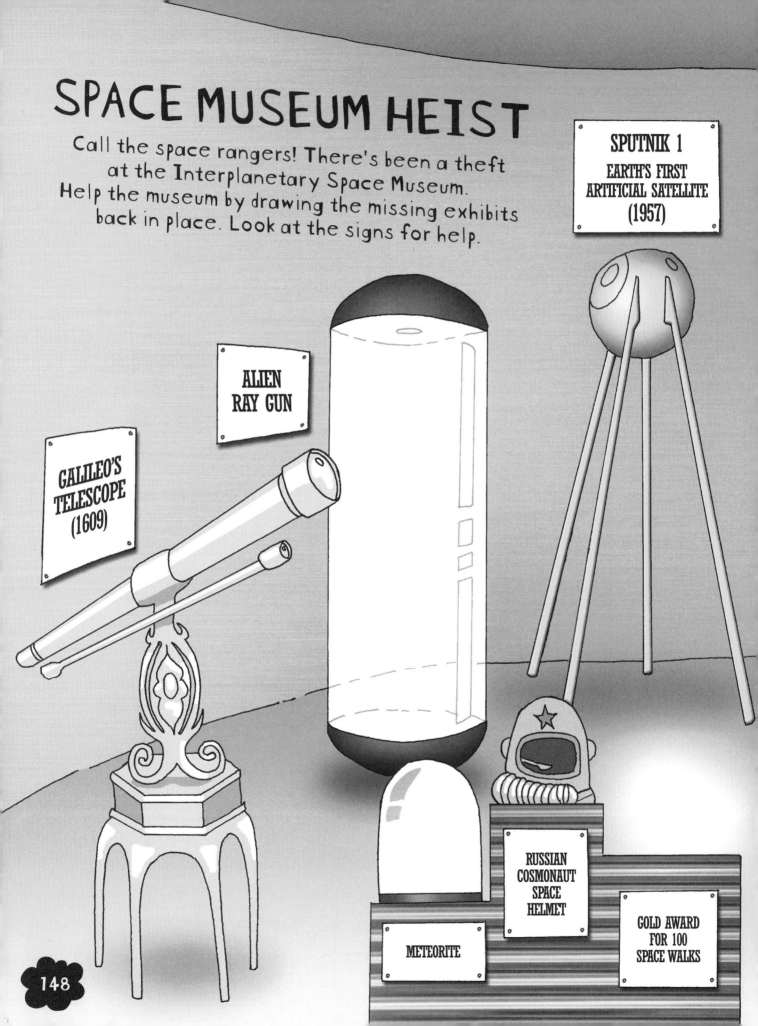

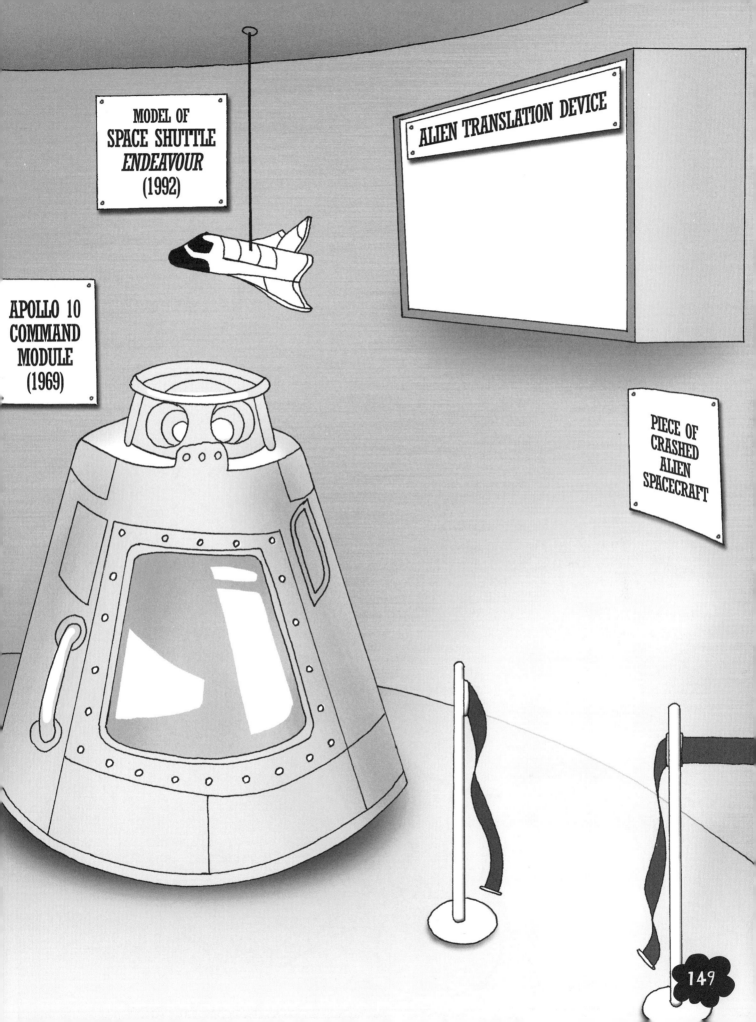

MODEL OF
SPACE SHUTTLE
*ENDEAVOUR*
(1992)

ALIEN TRANSLATION DEVICE

APOLLO 10
COMMAND
MODULE
(1969)

PIECE OF
CRASHED
ALIEN
SPACECRAFT

# what are they saying?

The wicked queen, disguised as an old woman, is trying to sell Snow White a poisoned comb. Write in what you think she is saying.

Colour in the pictures!

What is Snow White saying?

# Top ten excuses

Ten things Snow White could have said to the wicked queen to refuse the poisoned apple.

1. No thanks. I've just had my lunch.

2. I'm allergic to fruit.

3. Apple skin gets in my teeth.

4. Apples bring me out in spots.

5. Do you have a licence to sell fresh produce, Madam?

6. You look hungrier than me. I'll give you the money if you eat the apple.

7. I had a bad experience eating an apple once. I'll never do it again.

8. No speak English.

9. Gotta go! My bath is running.

10. Quick, get out of here! There's an apple-loving monster living in these woods.

Now make up your own excuse!

.....................................................................................

# A day at the races

Draw some magnificent hats onto the racegoers below, then colour in their outfits.

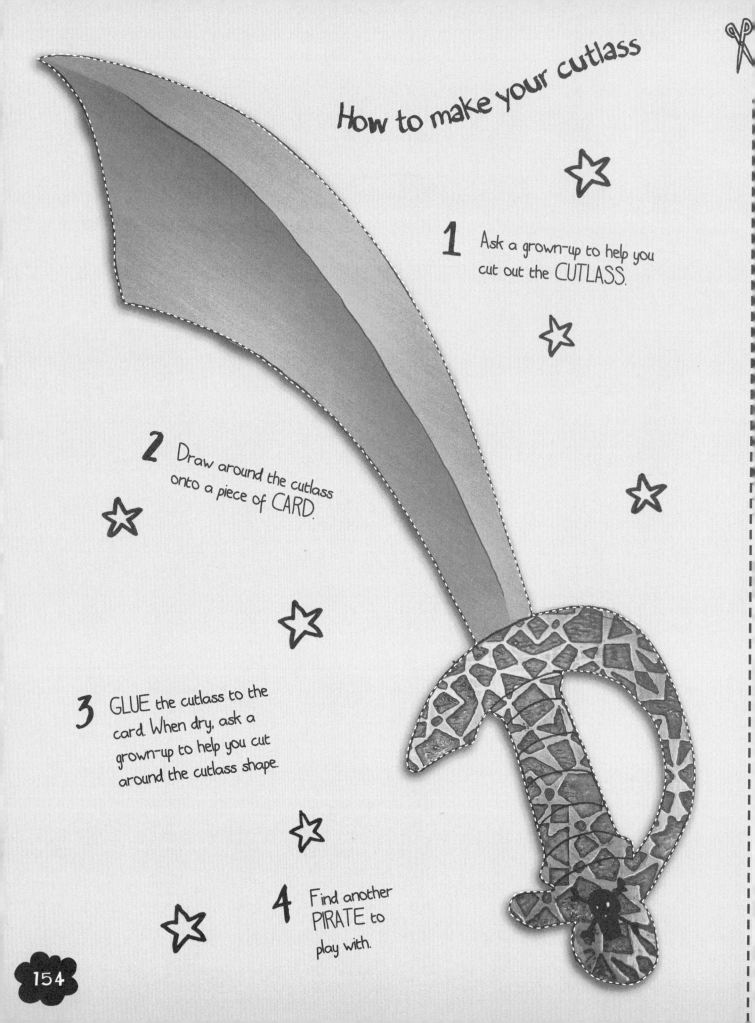

How to make your cutlass

**1** Ask a grown-up to help you cut out the CUTLASS.

**2** Draw around the cutlass onto a piece of CARD.

**3** GLUE the cutlass to the card. When dry, ask a grown-up to help you cut around the cutlass shape.

**4** Find another PIRATE to play with.

# Pirate talk

## Complete the phrases using the pirate words below.

1. (Two pirates greeting each other)  _ _ _ _  there, me hearties !

2. Bring the prisoners ! It's time to  _ _ _ _ _ / _ _ _ _ / _ _ _ _

3. What do pirates love more than anything?  _ _ _ _ _

4. Let's grab some grog and  _ _ _ _ _ _ _ _ / _ _ _ _ / _ _ _ _ _ _ _ _ _

5. You varmint! You're going to  _ _ _ _ _ / _ _ _ _ _ _ _ / _ _ _ _ _

PIRATE WORDS AND WHAT THEY MEAN...

Davy Jones's locker
(the bottom
of the sea)

Ahoy
(hello!)

booty
(stolen treasure)

feed the fish
(be thrown into
the sea)

splice the mainbrace
(take a drink)

Answers are at the back of the book.

155

# Seeing double

There are **12** differences. Can you spot the lot?

Answers are at the back of the book.

# How to dress your Stage School stars.

**1** Pull this page out of your book.

**2** Stick your stars to a piece of stiff card, then get a grown-up to help you cut them out.

**3** Next, cut out the clothes shapes on the back of your Stage School paper (page 159).

**4** Wrap the clothes you want to use round the dolls. Use the paper tabs to hold them in position.

**5** Make your own card doll shapes and stage clothes.

Take a look in a real mirror...

...then draw your reflection in this one.

# Fashion disasters

## What are these crazy people saying?

# VAMPIRE BITES

Expecting a houseful of horrors?
These savoury and sweet treats should keep
them from feasting on you.

## MUMMY'S FINGERS

INGREDIENTS:
Hot dogs, puff pastry, ketchup.

YOU WILL NEED:
Rolling pin, parchment paper,
baking sheet.

1. Wrap thin strips of ready-made
puff pastry round hot dogs to
look like bandages.

2. Place them on baking paper
on a baking sheet.

3. Ask a grown-up to bake them in the
oven for about 30 minutes, following
the instructions on the pastry pack.

4. When they are cooked cut them
in half crosswise and add a dab of
ketchup to the chopped end
to look like blood.

## Skeleton Cookies

INGREDIENTS:
Gingerbread cookie dough mix,
white icing.

YOU WILL NEED:
Rolling pin, gingerbread man cookie
cutter, baking paper, baking sheet,
decorating bag.

1. Roll out a sheet of cookie dough,
about 1 cm thick.

2. Use the cookie cutter to
shape several figures.

3. Place them on parchment paper
on a baking sheet.

4. Ask a grown-up to bake them in the
oven, following the instructions on
the cookie dough pack.

5. When the gingerbread men are
baked leave them to cool.

6. Put the icing into a decorating bag,
then decorate the cookies with skulls
and bones to give each gingerbread
man a skeleton.

## Witch's Hat Surprises

INGREDIENTS:
Small chocolate ice-cream cones,
chocolate iced cookies,
small sweets, icing.

YOU WILL NEED:
Decorating bag.

1. Fill a cone with small sweets.
Cover the open edge of the cone
with icing.

2. Carefully push the chocolate side
of the cookie onto the icing
cone to make a brim and glue the
two pieces together.

3. Turn the cone-and-cookie hat
over so the cookie is on the bottom.
Add more icing around the cone's base
to hold the parts together and make a
ribbon or buckle pattern.

# Camping chaos

Write a story to connect these crazy camping pictures.

It all started on a blustery day...

 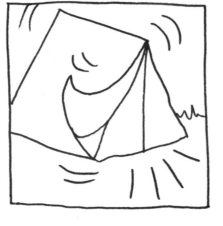 

———————————————   ———————————————   ———————————————

———————————————   ———————————————   ———————————————

———————————————   ———————————————   ———————————————

———————————————   ———————————————   ———————————————

The end

# Castle count-up

This poor tour guide is supposed to be showing 10 visitors round the castle, but the group has split up!

Can you help him find his lost guests?

Draw a circle around every tourist that you find.

THE METAL GRILLE AT THE ENTRANCE TO A CASTLE IS CALLED A PORTCULLIS.

The answer is at the back of the book.

# It's bedtime!

## Follow the lines to see which bed belongs to which dwarf.

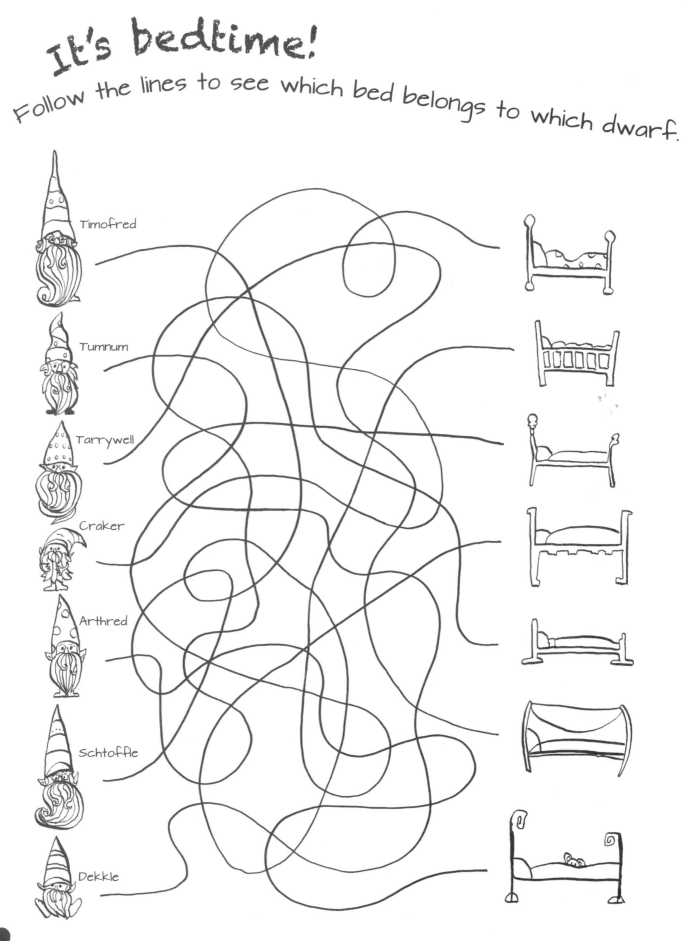

Timofred

Tumnum

Tarrywell

Craker

Arthred

Schtoffle

Dekkle

The answer is at the back of the book

# Pick up your pickaxe

Hidden in this picture are the dwarfs' seven pickaxes. When you find them colour them in.

The answer is at the back of the book

MY FIRST ROCKET

TRAINING

# SPACE SNAPS

Ray is telling stories about his time as an astronaut (again). But some of his photos are starting to fade.

Help Ray by colouring them in.

TRUCKING ON THE MOON

MISSION LAUNCH

MY FIRST SPACE WALK

MARS 1 CREW

LIFE ON MARS?

# Squares for Pirate doodles

# WANTED

Complete this picture of the world's most wanted pirate.
Follow the description below or make up a pirate face of your own.

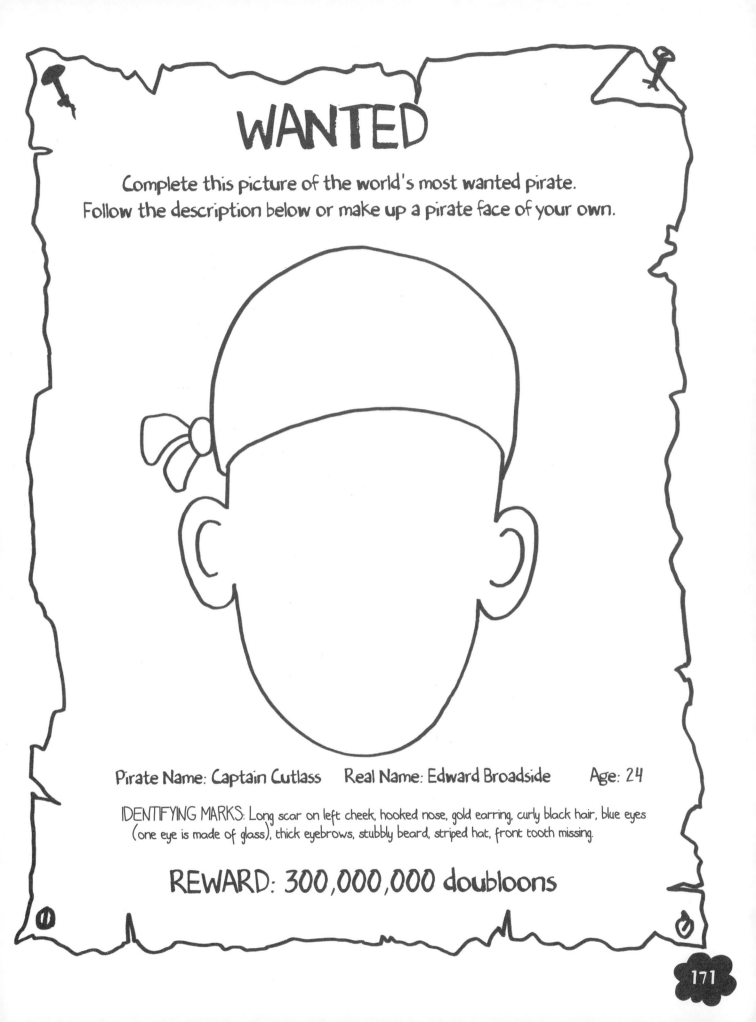

Pirate Name: Captain Cutlass     Real Name: Edward Broadside          Age: 24

IDENTIFYING MARKS: Long scar on left cheek, hooked nose, gold earring, curly black hair, blue eyes
(one eye is made of glass), thick eyebrows, stubbly beard, striped hat, front tooth missing.

## REWARD: 300,000,000 doubloons

# Dragon anatomy

This means body bits ↙

leathery wings ↓

horrible horns ↓

scary smoke ↙

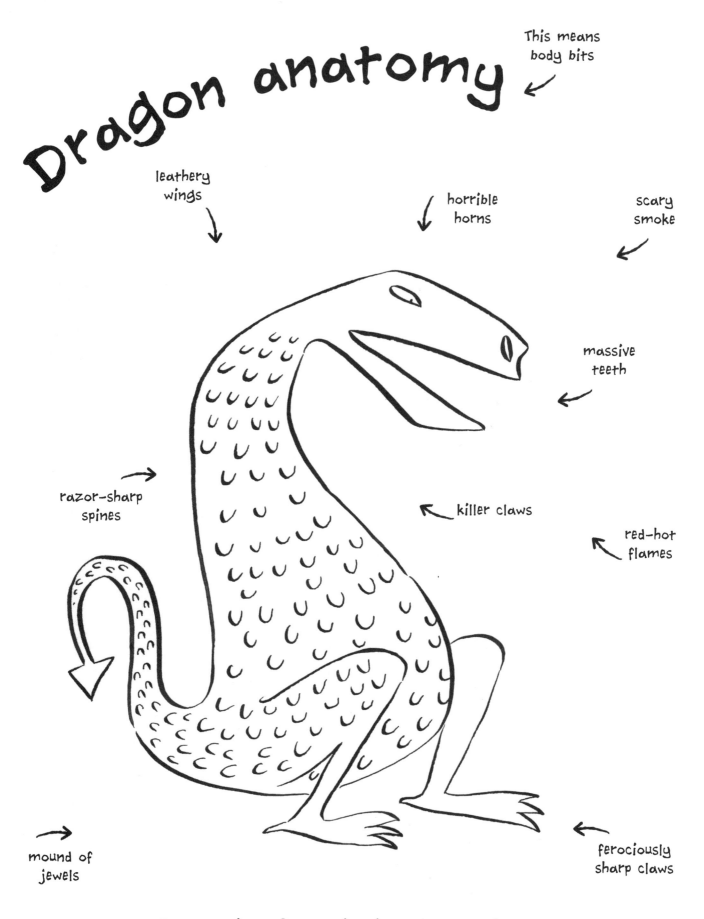

massive teeth ←

razor-sharp spines →

killer claws ←

red-hot flames ←

mound of jewels →

ferociously sharp claws ←

## Draw in the missing BODY parts.

# Down at the talon Salon

How would you like your NAILS done today?

# SIX FEET UNDER

Tell everyone you're not to be disturbed
while you work on this great gravestone craft.

## YOU WILL NEED:

Cereal box, pencil, scissors, newspaper, sticky tape, toilet paper,
glue mix (white glue mixed with half as much water),
brush, black and white paints, paintbrush

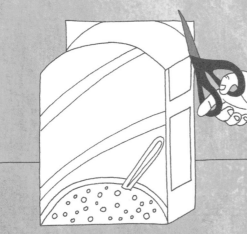

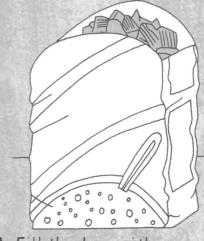

1. Draw an arch across the top
of the box, then carefully snip
the front and back of the box to
follow this shape.

2. Fill the box with scrunched-up
balls of newspaper, and squeeze
the box to give it a slightly
crumpled appearance.

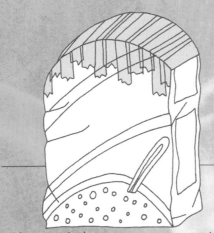

3. Use sticky tape to seal the top
of the box, following the arched
shape you drew.

4. Brush the box all over with the
glue mix and lay strips of toilet
tissue over the top. Do this over
and over again, until you have
about six slightly soggy layers.

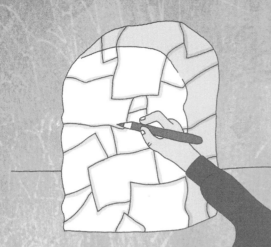

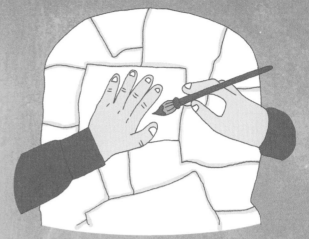

5. While the layers of paper are still damp, etch your gravestone message, using a pencil to scrape away some of the paper.

You could write "(YOUR NAME) only sleeping", "Here lies (YOUR NAME). Wake me up on Halloween" or "Beware! Future zombie!"

6. When you've finished writing, add one more layer of glue and tissue, and leave it to dry.

7. Paint your gravestone by dabbing on patches of black and white paint to give it the appearance of old stone. Use black paint inside your scraped message.

# Who's that girl?

Join the dots to find out what role this actress is playing.

The answer is at the back of the book.

# picture perfect

Copy this street dancer into the empty frame.

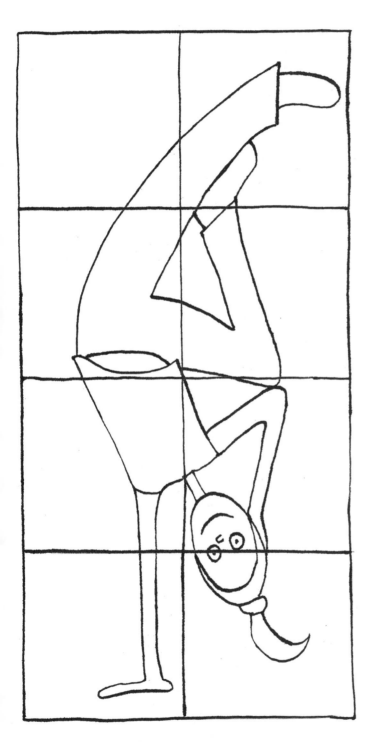

Try drawing one square a time.

# Work of art

What great work of art do you think these tourists are jostling to get a look at?

THE FAMOUS LOUVRE MUSEUM IN PARIS, FRANCE HOUSES ALMOST 35,000 OBJECTS AND WORKS OF ART.

Draw it in here.

# Lazy gazing

Circle eight differences between these rockpool pictures.

One of these marine moochers only appears in the top picture. Which is it?

sea urchin

hermit crab

starfish

The answers are at the back of the book.

# Decorate a shoe

Colour in some daring designs on these fabulous shoes.

# Escape!

Help Snow White through the woods. Starting in the centre, answer the questions and follow the arrows to find an escape route.

She loses a shoe and the path disappears. She has to go back to where she started.

Oh no! The raven causes a rock slide. Snow White is trapped! Only the seven dwarfs can save her.

Congratulations, you've led Snow White straight to the dwarfs' house.

YES

No, she runs away, back to where she started.

YES

No, she should stay on the path.

She comes to a fast-flowing stream. Should she hop over the stepping stones?

The raven flies to a cave and says that safety lies on the other side. Should she go in?

YES

LEFT

Into the trees

Which way should Snow White go?

Towards the clearing

She comes across a raven who says he'll help her out of the woods. Should she follow him?

She meets a friendly fox who tells her to go down the right path. Which path should she take?

No, she runs back to the trees.

YES

On the path she meets a suspicious old woman who tells her there's danger ahead. Should she turn back?

No, she should go on.

RIGHT

No, she should go back to the right path.

She comes to a rope bridge across a deep ravine, but it looks unstable. Should she cross it?

YES

The bridge collapses and she falls off. She has to climb back up to the path.

182

# Anyone home?

Join the dots to see where the dwarfs live.

Now colour it in! →

The answer is at the back of the book

# The Pirate King

Complete the picture.

This evil PIRATE KING has lost some of his most treasured possessions. Draw them in for him before he sets sail with all his dastardly pirate mates.

pirate hat

beard

parrot

cutlass

dagger

loyal dog

treasure chest

# Pirate things to colour in

coins

dagger

tropical island

pirate boot

hook

ship's wheel

cannon

eye patch

treasure chest

grog

ship

# GO, ROVER!

Copy each square of this drawing of the Mars Curiosity rover in the right order in the grid opposite.

3C

2A

1D

2B

1A

3B

1C

4D

2D

4A

3D

4B

2C

1B

4C

3A

A B C D

1

2

3

4

A B C D

### DID YOU KNOW?
NASA's *Curiosity* rover is a robotic car-sized laboratory that successfully landed on the surface of Mars in August 2012. It is digging, drilling and testing rocks to look for evidence that Mars may have once supported life or could even still host it now.

# FIVE REASONS WHY I'M THE PERFECT ASTRONAUT

You've almost come to the end of your first space mission, so tell the Astro Agency why they should send you on more adventures.

**I learnt how to** _____
_____
_____

**On the spaceship I** _____
_____
_____

**On other planets I found** _____
_____
_____

**In a battle with space pirates I** _____
_____
_____

**When I met aliens I** _____
_____
_____

Congratulations! You've made it through astronaut school and safely to the edge of our galaxy!

# THE ASTRO AGENCY

## AWARDS

## TOP HONOURS

### FOR

## EXCELLENCE IN SPACE EXPLORATION

### BY ORDER OF

*Commander Sam Astro*

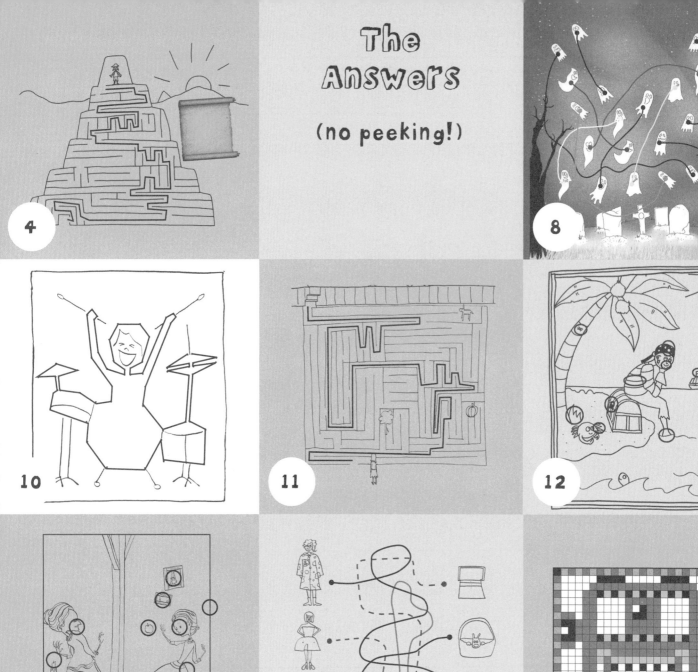

# The Answers

(no peeking!)

**4**

**8**

**10**

**11**

**12**

**29**

**30**

**33**

**34** The decoded message reads: Here lies Pharaoh Tut. Whoever disturbs his bones will be cursed by his undead soul.

**36**

**38**

**39** Third puzzle piece

**41**

**45**

1 Godfather should be godmother.
2 Blue should be Red; lion should be wolf.
3 Prince Calming should be Prince Charming.

**46**

5

**50**

**51**

**52**

Staying on a remote beach, far away from anyone. New Zealand is the best!

**56**

E: the animal is different.

**57**

**68**

Total = €6.15

**77**

**80**

34 bags

**110**

**111**
1. True (China)
2. False
3. True (Cambodia)
4. True (Vietnam)
5. False
   6. True
(Canada)

**123**

**133**
ASTEROID - True
BLACK HOLE - True
COMET - True
GALAXY - True
GIBBULON - False
LIGHT-YEAR - True
MILKY WAY - True
MOON - True
OBLONGON - False
SOLAR SYSTEM - Tr
STAR - True
SUPERNOVA - True
VORPAL DRIVE - Fals

**135**

**147**
1. Three
2. 09:24
3. 13:00

**155**
1. Ahoy  2. Feed the fish
3. Booty  4. Splice the
   mainbrace
5. Davy Jones's locker

**156**

**165**

**166**

**167**

**176**

**179**

**183**